JOYFUL COURAGE

Calming the Drama
and Taking
Control of *Your*
Parenting Journey

CASEY O'ROARTY, M.ED

For permission requests, write to the publisher, addressed "Attention: Permissions Coordinator," at the address below.

Alignment PUBLICATIONS

Alignment Publications

http://www.alignmentpub.com/

ISBN: (print): 978-1-7335715-0-0
ISBN: (ebook): 978-1-7335715-1-7

Ordering Information:
Special discounts are available on quantity purchases by corporations, associations, and others. For details, contact Alignment Publications at the address above.

Dedication

*To my mom. Thank you for the inspiration, the love,
the humility and the generosity you embody and share with
the people around you. I am so grateful for who we are together today
and for all the growing we will continue to do together tomorrow.*

*To Dad and Julie. Thank you for always believing in me,
and teaching me to work hard and reach for my dreams.*

*And to Ben, Rowan and Ian. Thank you for the grace,
compassion and daily opportunities to evolve into
a better version of myself. You are my favorites.*

Table of Contents

INTRODUCTION

Hey there. My name is Casey, and I am a mom, just like you.

I came into this parenting gig thinking that it would be so great, so easy. I figured I was at the perfect age, in a solid relationship with my husband, and we were both ready to jump into the next part of our life, so we went for it....

I had always been a kid person. I was a camp counselor, a babysitter, and went into teaching when I was 25 years old. Kids were my jam. I just got them.

And then I had my own.

From the start, I was surrounded by mamas that I looked up to. Mamas that introduced me to natural childbirth, attachment parenting, extended breastfeeding. Everything I learned in those early years felt instinctive to me. It felt right.

My first baby was like another limb. She spent a ton of time in the sling, riding along snug against me, no matter what event or experience was at hand. She nursed on demand and we co-slept. This worked for both my husband and me—we liked having her right there. We found our rhythm, and I learned to navigate the world with a baby, quickly forgetting what it was like "before."

Then I had my son. Hey, one is good, two is better, right?

I read a bit about the transition from one child to two, about the mama bear instinct to push your older child away. No way did I think this would be something that would happen to me. I was more concerned with how I could possibly love another child as deeply as I loved my first.

Then he arrived.

Wowzer—So. Much. Love.

And the mama bear instinct kicked in hard.

Those of you with more than one child know how it is. You have another baby and the older child becomes a giant overnight. And while I knew in my mind that she still needed me, this other, tiny, brand new human seemed to pull me right in. Turns out that I did, indeed, push my older child away. And it wasn't pretty.

It hurts to share that. I think about how confusing that must have been for her, all those years ago, when her mom changed so dramatically. My heart breaks as I wonder if some of the struggles she is dealing with today come from that early messaging and the experience of feeling like she didn't fit in the family.

I wasn't terrible all the time, but my threshold for what I could handle was low during those early years. I would snap and get mean. Mean to the girl that I loved the most, the one that made me a mother.

It was a dark time. But, what could I do? Like so many others, I was home all day with two little babies. It was both chaotic and monotonous.

Like there was no time and so much time. I felt guilty about not being grateful, and I would put on a brave face.

I loved those babies fiercely, of course. The pendulum would swing hard though, between the nurturing, connected, loving moments that we would share, and the angry, dysregulated, less than loving moments that we would live through.

During this same period of time, I was working on growing my parent education business—*ha!* I am sure you can imagine the conversations I had with myself around *that!* How could I stand up and speak to advise and support other parents when so much of my own parenting felt out of control?

In 2007, I decided that what I was doing clearly wasn't working for me. My daughter was picking on her little brother, and I was picking on her for picking on him, which led her to pick on him more. It was a disaster.

This is when I took the advice of a mama I love and admire deeply, and I looked up Positive Discipline. A month later, I was a trained Positive Discipline Parent Educator.

Learning the philosophy and practice of Positive Discipline, and facilitating others in learning about it, was a game changer for me. Not only did it shift the dynamics in my own family, and specifically my relationship with my daughter, but also it was a philosophy I was proud to share.

In the years that followed, the climate of our home shifted. My daughter and I were able to mend our relationship, and move forward in a connected and loving way. I learned to recognize how I was contributing to the dynamics that were happening in our home, and I learned strategies for creating an home environment that celebrated contribution, cooperation, and learning from mistakes.

Teaching parenting classes kept me in the practice of walking my talk—most of the time. It offered me a beautiful practice of accountability and personal responsibility for my actions. I was *not*, and *am* not, a perfect parent. I am a shit show a lot of the time. But I am aware of what is happening, and I am willing to be honest and vulnerable with my kids and with other parents. I am willing to get up and try again.

In 2011, I began to write about my parenting experiences in a blog. I found that it was helpful for me to tell my real and raw stories, and that it also helped others to read them and not feel so alone.

That blog evolved into a website, and in April of 2014, I published my first podcast. I am now over 150 shows in....

What has always been important to me is to hold space for parents to make sense of their journey. To help parents recognize that there is always room to grow, evolve, and expand as humans—and that our children chose us to light our way.

As of the writing of this book, my children are 12 and 15 years old. I remain in the thick of it, but I am stronger and more committed than ever to how I show up for them. The pendulum still swings, but the arch is much smaller.

Not only do I continue to facilitate parenting classes, I also speak at conferences, lead online workshops, and coach private clients, all with the intention of supporting other parents in being and growing into the best versions of themselves.

Parenting is no joke. I know I'm not the only one that assumed it would be easy, that I would be filled with love, that I'd enjoy *every precious moment* I could spend with my children.

And yes, there is love and joy. But there can also be levels of anger, fear, and frustration that we may never have known before.

It can take us by surprise.

Didn't know you were a complete control freak before you had kids? Neither did I.

In those moments of intense emotion, it can feel like our bodies have been taken over. We may say or do things that we never thought we would say or do. It can get ugly.

We all start off wanting to be "good moms" and "good dads"—only to find out we don't always know what that means. Challenges arise and it can feel like the wind is being knocked out of us. Our hopes of being a positive, conscious, intentional parent fly out the window.

It can be startling.

It can be painful.

It can leave us feeling hopeless and defeated.

This book is all about *how to navigate the challenges of raising children,* while choosing to be a connected human being. How to be engaged with the demands of parenting, without riding the emotional freight train. This book is about parenting with Joyful Courage.

Part One of this book will help you to get more familiar with your emotional freight train—what it is, how it feels, and the baggage and passengers that join you for the ride.

Part Two will help you to identify who you want to be as a parent, help you practice being that parent, and offer tools that will help you get off the train.

Part Three will help you to integrate and sustain those practices so you can live the life you want. We are imperfect. We will make mistakes. But there are ways to integrate the lessons from this book into your life so you'll be more likely to show up as a present, courageous, joyful parent.

But **What Is** Joyful Courage?

In 2012, Joyful Courage was simply the name I chose for my business. I love those two words together. I love to think that being brave, stepping into courage, can be a *joyful* experience.

A few years later I ran a couple of programs online that really took off and nurtured a mighty group of mamas. They were thrilled to learn tools for being in a relationship with their children, while also growing themselves. They began to speak of Joyful Courage as a concept.

And why wouldn't it be a concept?

For a few years now, I have asked my podcast guests, "What does Joyful Courage mean to you?" I love the variety of answers that show up. I love to hear the people that inspire me speak in to their own definitions of Joyful Courage.

Recently I have come to realize that it is time for *me* to define what Joyful Courage means.

The era of parenting I am now in lends itself perfectly to what Joyful Courage means. My children are beginning their journeys of navigating middle and high school. I am coming to realize that nothing can really prepare you for watching your children struggle with all the challenges that come with adolescence. I am being called into some deep work as fear and a sense of losing control bubble up inside me....

When I can pull up and out of my experience, when I can look *at* what is happening with my kids, instead of *from* it, I have a broader perspective. I can see that my role in all of this is to love them and to get out of their way. I am also experiencing, while writing this book, how challenging that can be.

I believe that our children choose us. That even before we come into these physical bodies, our spirits make agreements about what we are meant to teach each other through our human relationships and experiences. I believe that we are meant to evolve and expand each other as we navigate the world and all that crosses our path.

This gets me really fired up! And at the same time, it brings me a sense of peace because if this is true, if children are meant to teach us, then there is a purpose to the path. And purpose gives me something to anchor into, especially in times of high stress and fear.

So, the definition that I have landed on is that Joyful Courage is "*rejoicing in the opportunities for personal growth and development on the parenting journey, while creating a home environment steeped in love, learning, and connection.*"

Joyful Courage is taking a pause, finding perspective, and parenting in a way that maintains the relationship with the human in front of you, while also connecting with the learning that your child is inviting you into.

Joyful Courage parenting is parenting *on purpose*.

It is thoughtful.

It is respectful.

It is being confronted by a child having a hard time and choosing to show up in a way that is helpful and not hurtful.

Joyful Courage is *trusting* yourself and your intuition, even when it feels hard to do.

Joyful Courage parents have decided who they want to be, and they practice that way of being on a regular basis so they can access it when they need to. When it really counts.

It isn't easy. It's messy! We are emotional beings in a relationship with other emotional beings who have *very limited life skills.* It can feel like a straight up shit show sometimes.

This book is going to help you with that.

When we take the time to *choose* the way we show up, to *choose* a way of being that will serve us and the relationships we have with the people we love, we can be better for ourselves and our children, *even when it is hard.*

I promise you, it's worth it. I hope you will join me.

PART ONE

All Aboard!

You've Found Yourself on the Emotional Freight Train!

Welcome! You've taken the first step. You have allowed your curiosity to guide you to purchasing this book. Well done.

Part One of this book will support you in deepening your understanding of the emotional freight train, what makes yours unique to you, and the triggers that pull it into the station.

You will hear from members of the Joyful Courage community speaking into their experiences, and my guess is that you will connect with their sharing.

This is big work. This is an opportunity to look inward at how our toughest moments are effecting the way we feel and think about ourselves and our family. These are places we often avoid, but I invite you to lean in. I invite you to be willing to learn and grow. I will be with you every step of the way.

CHAPTER ONE

I Cannot Believe I Just Did That!

What Is the Emotional Freight Train?

You know that moment when you go from calm and happy to totally pissed off? When you find yourself blaming, shaming, or criticizing others? When your body is hot and tense, and logic has left the building?

Yeah, that moment.

That's your emotional freight train.

When you go from being totally Zen and present to irrational and mean? Yup, that's it too.

We all have visits from the emotional freight train. Some of us have trains that pull up slow and give us all sorts of signals that it's about to pull into the station. Some of us have trains that zoom in, leaving us no time to prepare.

Let me tell you a story about one of my own emotional freight train experiences (one of many...)

Years ago, we would take the kids, Rowan and Ian, up skiing at our local mountain on Sunday mornings. They were doing a six-week ski lesson program and this particular day was the morning of week five. When we got up to the parking lot, my son, Ian, who was six at the time, was really dragging his feet and didn't want to get his gear on. As my husband helped our daughter get ready, I tried to engage Ian to move along.

He wasn't having it. "I don't want to go," was what he said, scowling at me with his arms crossed so I'd know that he meant it.

I went to the back of the car and told my husband to take Rowan up to the ski area, and that I was going to sit in the car with Ian and give him some space and time to work it out. We had an hour before lessons started, plenty of time

Once Ben and Rowan started to walk away from the car, Ian's meltdown began to escalate. I have a hard time remembering now exactly what the problem was to begin with, but it quickly became about wanting daddy to help him get ready. *Let him have his emotions,* I kept saying to myself, *don't get dragged in...*I told him I was happy to help him get his gear on, and to let me know when he was ready. He just continued to cry and whine, saying he wanted daddy to come back, that he didn't want to do ski lessons, that Rowan could stay up there by herself....This went on for a looooong time.

And for a long while, I was able to maintain my calm. I was able to keep things steady on the outside, even as the tension in my body grew. Was he ever going to get over this? Didn't he see how hard I was working to stay compassionate and available? Did he think I *liked* sitting in the car listening to him howl? Who the hell did he think he was??

Then finally it happened—I lost it.

I reached back and took a firm grip on his leg, and I said, in my meanest mommy voice, "Knock it off! You are acting like a spoiled brat!" There it was, my breaking point. I could feel the heat in my body, the lack of control. I sprung like a snake that had been coiled and waiting to attack. I totally lost my shit. And once I lost it, it was like I gave myself over to my emotions.

Ian, of course, was sent into a much bigger meltdown—crying in disbelief and hurt. "*I'm not acting like a spoiled brat!*" he hollered at me, the wild look in his eyes matching my own.

Did I retreat? No. I did get a bit calmer, but I launched into what I thought he needed to hear: "Kids that are spoiled only think about themselves. You expect daddy to come back down here after he has already walked all the way to the ski hill. You expect Rowan to wait around up there by herself because you want daddy. You don't care that I am sitting here waiting to help you as soon as you're ready—you are only thinking about you and what you want..." *Blah, blah, blah, blah....*

This was the emotional freight train. I had felt it pull in: The tension that was building in my body was a signal that the train was on its way. When I snapped, that was me hopping on, letting go of being the designer of my experience and handing over the controls. And as it does, the emotional freight train headed straight into victim town. I was there. I was pissed and I was blaming my son for his lack of perspective, compassion, and respect for others.

Did I mention he was six?

And oh man, he was mad—and why shouldn't he be? I am the mom, the one who needs to be the adult, emotionally available to my kids—and yet I met *his* meltdown with *my own* meltdown. I was overwhelmed by my inability to control the situation and I snapped. Did it help him to feel better? No. Did it help him learn to self-soothe? No. He was hurt and he was mad at me. There was no self-reflection there—just anger that mommy could be so mean.

Eventually, he crawled into the back of the van and started to get his gear on. He didn't ask for help, just quietly got ready. I gave him some space and after a few minutes I climbed back there too and I said, "I am sorry I got so mad at you. It didn't help you feel any better and it was a mistake for me to act like that. Can we hug it out?" He then turned to me and fell into my arms. I could have cried at the forgiveness I felt in that little embrace.

In the end, we were able to make amends and move on. But the weight I carried about how I reacted to my son that day was heavy in my heart for a long time.

The emotional freight train is ruthless.

I try and I try, and then I snap!

Like many of you reading this book, I have read a ton of blogs and books about parenting. I have also been trained in *two* different parenting practices! And while the philosophies and ideas that I learned really landed for me, I was still finding it challenging in the heat of the moment to respond in a way that was helpful and not hurtful....

Each night I would put my head on my pillow and promise myself that I would do better tomorrow. I declared: no yelling, more patience, more playfulness, and *more presence for God's sake!*

And then the next day would roll around and I would get caught in the same cycle of irritation and resentment. Maybe I would give those tools I knew about a try, but they just didn't seem to help, or they didn't match the real-life challenges that I was having with my kids—and so the emotional freight train would show up and take over. Again!

If you are nodding your head and saying "yes, yes, *yes*," know that you're *not* alone. We parents share a collective experience. I gathered stories from the Joyful Courage community about their experience with the emotional freight train, and I am guessing you will hear yourself in their shares:

> *"When my emotional freight train pulls up, I feel totally detached from my kid's experience. I'm in full reaction mode and I become bent on changing my child's behavior right then and there. My ability to see the situation is totally clouded—it's a blur, as if I'm speeding past it. I'm overcome with the urge to 'do something' to make the behavior stop. My emotions can range from fear to disbelief to pure anger.*
>
> *I'm responding from a place of shame—I feel like I must have failed to parent my children properly for them to behave in this way. Or I am hijacked by worry. I am overcome with an impulse to 'get my message across' right then. Usually this comes in the form of a lecture, and I find myself saying the same thing over and over. I think I'm subconsciously (and desperately) looking for the words that will result in my children saying, "Oh Mom, yeah, I get it! You're right, I won't do that again!"*
>
> *– Mama Christie P.*

> *"When my emotional freight train pulls up, I feel hot, irritated, angry, and sometimes hopeless. I immediately fall into all-or-nothing thinking, like 'They never listen to me' or 'I will always feel ignored' or 'This isn't how being a mother was supposed to be.'*

I begin to wonder why I can't seem to get it together, or why my kids can't get it together, and why everything seems so difficult. Other families seem to be able to go out to brunch without issue...what is wrong with my family!? When will I actually want to spend quality time with my kids, or will it always feel like something I have to brace myself for."

– Mama Lauren R.

"I feel out of control in my mind and chest. The anger rises up in me to a point where I cannot rationalize my thoughts enough to calm myself. I am thinking I am a horrible example to my kids and a bad mom."

– Mama Ana P.

"When my emotional freight train pulls in, I feel hot with adrenaline pumping, teeth grinding, jaw locked and tense, blood pumping. The emotions that show up vary—disbelief, incredulous, annoyed, hurt, frustrated..."

– Mama Liz N.

"When my emotional freight train pulls up, I feel a fire of emotion that rips through my body. I feel almost removed—like an observer of my experience unable to change course. Anger, frustration, fear, shame—they all seem to play into keeping my emotional freight train fuelled. In the moment, I embody the

feelings and allow them to follow their track. When we reach the end of the track and I am spent, I feel stuck, and doomed to continue this pattern. I fear my children will learn that staying on the train is okay. Or I think my children will learn to not respect me or value me because I cannot get it together."

– Mama Nelly B.

"I feel my body tighten, my shoulders get tense and my arms tuck in tight to my side, and I feel like I want to scream and yell. The emotions that show up are anger, disbelief, impatience, or frustration, and I am thinking I need to stop what my child is doing this instant. I am thinking I need to be scary so they will stop their misbehavior."

– Mama Tricia W.

You are not alone.

We all have visits from the emotional freight train. We *all* find ourselves with certain things that get under our skin, and push us out of our rational mind and into the emotional part of our brain.

When we're in the weeds, it can seem like the emotional freight train is impossible to avoid. We should be *enjoying* parenthood. It's supposed to be *the best part of our lives.*

Is it any wonder that we feel so shitty?

This book is going to help you.

I have been teaching and practicing Positive Discipline since 2007, and I founded my parent education business, Joyful Courage, in 2012. Because

Positive Discipline is a part of my foundation of parenting, I am going to take a little time right now to fill you in a bit on what it's all about. I have two children who are being raised in a Positive Discipline home.

Positive Discipline is a parenting program developed by Jane Nelsen. This program is based on the work of psychologists Alfred Adler and Rudolf Dreikurs, and it promotes the belief that behavior is based on the need for connection and knowing that we matter. The Positive Discipline parenting style is neither permissive nor authoritarian, instead, some call it democratic. It is founded on mutual respect, being kind *and* firm at the same time, learning from mistakes and using encouragement as a tool for supporting children to be their best selves.

Positive Discipline is all about teaching, modeling, and practicing life skills through life experience and inside of deeply connected relationships. As Jane Nelsen says in her book, *"Where did we ever get the crazy idea that in order to make children do better, first we have to make them feel worse? Children do better when they feel better."*

Positive Discipline shies away from the behaviorist practices of punishments and rewards, and instead looks through a different lens when considering behavior. As Adler found, *humans "move away" from feeling less than and "towards a sense of belonging and significance."*

Positive Discipline invites parents to look at the beliefs children have *behind* their behavior, and to support children in finding *solutions* to the problems and challenges they are facing, thus developing life skills along the way.

Easier said than done.

Positive Discipline, positive parenting, conscious parenting—it all seems so simple on paper, but it can feel messy when we are in the process of implementing it in our homes.

Even with everything I've practiced and learned, I can become triggered and emotional with my children. And I am *intimately* familiar with the emotional freight train, which is why I wanted to share my story, and what I have learned along the way, with you.

The articles and blogs we read just aren't enough to make the difference that *really* matters.

As I mention in the introduction, I teach classes both live and online. I taught at my local YMCA for years, and I've worked with hundreds of parents. Most of those parents have taken the learning and are practicing it successfully in their homes. But every once in a while, I run into a mom or a dad who has taken my class and they are frustrated. They tell me *"I love all the tools you share, but when anger takes over, I just can't seem to access them!"*

These parents are being picked up by the emotional freight train and are unable to find the controls to slow it down.

Getting off the emotional freight train starts with becoming more curious about the way you are reacting, paying more attention to your physical sensations, feelings, and thoughts, and learning more about yourself. This will help you get better at choosing different responses. It is about learning to broaden your perspective, about what is happening in the present moment.

As we carry on, you will read the stories of other parents who have immersed themselves in this work. Parents who were willing to look inward, to get clear how they were feeling during a powerful emotional response, and to recognize the ways they were unknowingly adding to the challenges they were experiencing with their children. You may see yourself in their stories—my hope is that you do.

The emotional freight train is real for all of us; it shows up and whisks us away, often without us being fully conscious of it. Choosing to find *your* Joyful Courage, choosing to learn and grow, and develop yourself as you navigate the emotional freight train (EFT) will bring you clarity and confidence on the journey.

The next chapter will challenge you to get a deeper understanding of what is happening on *your* EFT, and it will invite you to discover places where you can begin to shift your way of thinking about behavior, both your kids' behavior and your own.

CHAPTER TWO

What Exactly is Happening on Your Emotional Freight Train?

At the beginning of parenting classes, I start by asking, *"What are the challenges you are experiencing in your home?"*

People tend to generate the same list, no matter if I am talking to parents in the city or the country, or to parents of toddlers, elementary schoolers, or teenagers—it's always the same.

Whining

Tantrums

Back talk

Not listening

Disrespect

Picky eating

Fighting

Negotiating

Swearing

Screen time drama ¯

Bedtime/morning drama

Lying

Biting/hitting/kicking

Sibling conflict

The list goes on....

Positive Discipline educators and trainers *all over the world* ask this question and the answers are consistent. Then the energy in the room shifts as parents look around and smile at each other. They realize they're not alone.

For me, the things that are currently triggers are the "I know everything there is to know about everything and you know nothing" attitude of my teenagers, as well as their insatiable desire to be on their phones. Also, the eye rolling, the angsty response to simple requests, and the power struggles that crop up, forcing me to confront the fact that I actually can't control everything my children do.

It's so annoying.

I asked the Joyful Courage community about what triggers them most. Here's what I heard:

> *"Defiance—especially when partnered with rudeness. An outright 'No, I'm not going to do that' can leave me feeling desperate, out of control, and immediately drawn into a power struggle.*

Unkind behavior is also huge for me. If I see my child behaving unkindly towards a friend or sibling, I am filled with worry, shame, and disappointment."

– Mama Christie P.

"When my husband and kids are talking to me at the same time and both need my attention without being aware of the other. I become overwhelmed and feel the heat rising from my chest all the way to my head."

– Mama Ana P.

"Big negative emotions, such as anger and frustration, interrupting, disrespectful behavior, such as name calling or hitting, and overwhelmed due to a lot of noise and distraction during busy times of the day, such as when making dinner or trying to get out the door in the morning."

– Mama Amber F.

"When others, children and adults, are inconsiderate of others' needs or feelings, when children or adults behave in selfish ways, when I am feeling overwhelmed with tasks, to-dos, and chores. When I am feeling alone in the act of never-ending parental decision making, and fearful that this one decision about something mundane could come back to haunt me. When I hear whining

and complaining. When they're not willing to try something new or to keep an open mind."

– Mama Justine S.

It's a collective experience.

Your freakshow may take on a slightly different flavor than your neighbor's freakshow, but you can be sure that we are all challenged as parents. We all have children who trigger us left and right.

This is important to understand. Much of what is happening in your home, in my home, is par for the course. Many of us parents (myself included) fall into the trap of judging ourselves, judging our children, and judging our family on the challenges that show up.

It can sound like this:

My toddler is having a meltdown because I won't buy him what he wants. *He is so entitled—what am I doing wrong?*

My daughter won't do her homework. *She doesn't care about her education; I am failing her.*

My family can't get through a dinner together without arguing. *This is so dysfunctional; why don't we have it together?*

I just busted my teenager vaping. *I've picked the wrong parenting style; she's sure to be a statistic now….*

The freakshow happens. Our inner conversation takes over. *Enter the emotional freight train.*

Sometimes while dealing with the challenges mentioned above, parents may appear outwardly calm but their tone and words are hurtful. Other times their response can be explosive. Either way, the train can usher in more thoughts that spin us into fear and anger.

This isn't helpful.

Toddlers have meltdowns. It's not because they are entitled little brats but because they have limited skills. They're learning how to navigate the flood of emotions caused by disappointments. Not because the parent has done anything wrong.

Sometimes kids resist homework because they don't see the value in it for them (and many educators and parents share this opinion—but that is another book). It has nothing to do with us *failing* them.

Families argue at dinner for a variety of reasons, including everyone (grownups and kids) wanting to be heard. Not because your family is dysfunctional.

And finally, teenagers are going to do stupid, *stupid* things, regardless of the parenting style we choose in the first 12 years. Their brains are still developing. They are going to be okay.

Can we influence the above situations? Heck yes, we can. In fact, I would argue that we are always influencing the events and experiences we have. We either make it worse or we make it better. The more aware we become of our internal struggles while we're experiencing them, the more intentional we can be in how we influence the outcome.

What is the internal struggle and how do we become more aware of it?

I think we can all agree that there is the world that exists outside of us, and the world that exists inside of us. On the outside, people are saying and doing things, events are occurring, things are happening. On the inside, we are making meaning and judgements, experiencing emotions and self-talk, making decisions, all in response to what is happening on the outside.

When you start to pay attention, internally, to the meaning you are making, to the judgment and the self-talk that is fueling your emotions and decision making, you begin to see that there is a lot of room to help yourself experience the outside world differently.

This is a human experience, right? It's not only about our children. Think about a time when you have to share something with a friend or your partner. Maybe you're venting about a big project, or even something like laundry. Imagine saying, "Oh man, the laundry! I am so over it! Every day there is more to do. It's so annoying! I am just not going to do it anymore. Screw it!"

Now imagine the other person responds, "How can you not see how important keeping up with the laundry is? Don't you care about your family? Their well being? If you don't do the laundry, your children will go to school in dirty clothes; they will start to get teased. Next thing you know they will be victims of online bullying and eventually choose to self-harm."

How would you respond? Maybe you'd respond with "Calm down. I'm just venting my frustration." Or maybe even "OMG, are you not hearing me? I just said I don't like laundry!" Or perhaps you're just thinking *dang, this isn't a person who I can trust to share my pain with.*

I know, that is a little extreme. But don't we do this with our kids? They say something like, "I hate my brother" and we jump all over them about all the reasons they should love their brother, and we follow up with, "and we don't use the word hate in this family." We completely miss the opportunity to hear about what is actually going on for them!

Go back to the laundry story and imagine that it is a conversation between you and your teenager. They are letting you know how they feel about doing their own laundry, and you are the one letting them know that they will ultimately end up as losers in life if they don't do it. Motivation? Not so much.

Your response matters.

Your response to the parenting freakshow is where you hold power to influence the outcome. When you respond from a conscious, grounded, connected place, the results of your interaction will lean more towards conscious, grounded, and connected relationships.

Does that make sense? I know it can get confusing. What I am *not* saying is that there is some magical way to get the outcome you want. This is not about blind obedience. We are *in relationships*. And when you consider that one day our children will be looking toward their peers and partners for advice or opinions, blind obedience tends to lose its luster.

What I *am* saying is that the way we respond to the challenges of our life, whether with our children or other adults, has a direct impact on how things play out. When we are paying attention to our emotions, our inner dialogue, the fears and control that can show up (a.k.a., the emotional freight train)—and we can shift to a place that is more centered and connected—we are going to get to the other side of the situation with our relationship intact. People hear and see each other better when they aren't freaking out and stuck in their own perspective.

It's kind of like a backdoor way of increasing the likelihood that your child ends up a responsible, contributing member of society, right?

This is something that I am constantly working on with my teenage daughter. She throws all sorts of things at me, all day long—things that hook me and challenge me, and sometimes just plain *baffle* me. She is sharing her thoughts and feelings in the moment, and often I forget that ultimately she just wants me to see her and hear her, and maybe to go under the surface to explore what the real issue is.

A lot of the time, what she is saying has *nothing* to do with what is really going on for her in the moment.

For example, there was a time when she asked if she could go spend some time with a friend of hers on a Friday night. This friend is a boy, and a kid that I know has gotten into some trouble. He's been to our house and I genuinely like him. When she asked if she could hang out with him, however, I gave her the third degree, triggered by my fear and worry that she might get into mischief.

The train pulled into the station. It was subtle, but it was there.

The message she heard was "I don't trust you."

As I tried to make logical arguments as to why I wanted to just be a "no" to this request, she blurted out in a voice full of defiance that she didn't want to go to counseling anymore (she had been twice).

There it was—her bid for control and influence in the midst of my fear-based tirade.

And boy, she got me. I had been encouraging her to go to a counselor for months and she had finally agreed. She knew how thrilled I was that she was willing to go, and it was the perfect thing to throw at me in that moment. She was feeling hurt and controlled, so she let me know how little control I actually had.

Fortunately, I had been doing my work. Meaning, I recognized this comment for what it was and didn't get hooked into a big explosion of "Oh yes you will…"

Instead, I took a deep breath and let her know that I was walking away from the conversation for a bit. I acknowledged that we weren't done talking, but I wanted to calm down so that we could continue the conversation in a way that was helpful for us both.

In that moment, the train came to a screeching halt, and I stepped off.

When we are on the emotional freight train, we don't respond from a conscious place.

The next sections will guide you in getting ever more familiar with what is happening *to you* as you respond to the freakshow that triggers you *out* of conscious parenting, away from positive parenting, and into crazy parent mode.

Getting familiar with our bodies.

Our bodies hold a lot of information. Our bodies are wise. Our bodies don't filter things the way our minds do. Our bodies are nonjudgmental. Our bodies tell us the truth.

This is by design. For the first humans, survival was an everyday challenge. They had to be on guard and paying attention to threats from the outside world. This is the fight-or-flight response, and it is a physiological response to the world around us, sending us into appropriate action when threatened—fight, run, or freeze to be a less visible target.

But even more important to note is that as soon as the brain takes in a perceived threat, it sends messages and adrenaline to the body and moves it into action, even before we are aware of what is happening.

We literally move from our logical brain into our emotional/survival brain in a matter of seconds, and the only clues we have that we are there is the way our body is responding.

For more information about our brain's fight or flight response, check check out Dr. Dan Seigel's *Brain in the Palm of the Hand* video, plus others, at www.joyfulcourage.com/eftbook.

When I was in the conversation with my daughter that I mentioned earlier, my body told me when fear had shown up—a sharp inhale of breath, a tense jaw, a tight belly. There was no story to try and make sense of—it was purely physical sensation. It was a fight-or-flight response. My body was sharing information with me.

When we decide to practice conscious parenting—parenting with awareness and Joyful Courage—it's essential for us to get familiar with how our bodies respond to emotions and triggers. When we pay attention to the *physical* experience we have when we are triggered, we see patterns. We begin to recognize that our bodies know when we are about to get on the train, and our bodies know when we decide to go along for the ride.

What do I mean by the "physical experience?"

Think about the last time your child triggered you and you fell apart. What did your legs feel like? What about your face? What can you remember about your shoulders and your chest? Did you feel heat? Where did you feel tension?

If you can't remember, pay attention next time. Pay attention to what happens to your body—the physical sensations, the tension, your posture.

I experience tension. My jaw, shoulders, and belly tighten. I inhale and then hold my breath. My heart starts to race. I lean forward and pull my shoulders in. I take the fighter's stance.

When I am paying attention, I can feel myself going there. I can feel the tension. I can tell when I am heading towards being triggered. Most of the time.

Have you ever walked into your child's room and looked around in disgust? Disgust, along with fear and anger, is one of the emotions that takes people to that fight-or-flight place. Disgust can be an invitation to the emotional freight train. This happens to me when I walk into my son's room. This may sound familiar to you, but my son takes his clothes off and leaves them wherever they fall. He also opens drawers to pick out clothes and doesn't bother to close the drawers.

Makes. Me. Crazy.

Walking into that room at the end of the evening, when all he wants is some love and connection, my whole body tightens at the sight of the clothes and the drawers. Tight shoulders, tight jaw, and ready to lay into him about his room.

What I practice is to notice that tension, notice the tightness, and breathe through it. Sometimes I kick all the clothes into a pile and close the drawers, and sometimes I invite *him* to do it, but no matter what I decide to do, I am aware that my body is giving me signals that the train has pulled in. And this awareness is helping me stay off the train more often.

What does *your* physical experience of stress feel like? Responses from parents I have coached include:

"When my emotional freight train pulls up, I feel hot, irritated, angry, and sometimes hopeless."

"I feel out of control in my mind and chest."

"When my emotional freight train pulls in, I feel hot with adrenaline pumping, teeth grinding, jaw locked and tense, blood pumping."

"I feel tight and hot."

"I feel as though my body shrinks and my head swells."

"I feel my body tighten, my shoulders get tense, and my arms tuck in tight to my side, and I feel like I want to scream and yell."

Becoming familiar with how our bodies respond to emotional overwhelm is key to staying off the train. A tantrum-ing toddler is not the same as an attacking bear, though it can sure feel that way.

While our brain's wiring kept our ancestors alive, it can get in the way now, especially when the perceived "threat" is our children. Our safety instincts don't serve us the way they used to. When we learn how this instinct works inside of us, we can get better at overriding it. That will support us with being more helpful and connected with our children.

Pay attention to your body's response. Write down what you experience each time. Look for your pattern. Notice the subtle shifts and changes. What are your clues?

Exploring the stories we are telling ourselves.

The emotional freight train hijacks our body.

But it doesn't stop there. When we're triggered, our minds also take on a life of their own. This is where we start future tripping. Our body is tense and all we are left with is "I need to shut this behavior down *now*, or else."

This is where we become hypercritical of ourselves and our children. This is when our perception of other people's judgment takes the driver's seat. We spin out.

Again, from the Joyful Courage community:

"I am thinking I am a horrible example to my kids and a bad mom."

"The emotions are anger and overwhelm, and I'm thinking that I can't handle this and I feel like my kids are the enemy."

"I have thoughts such as, 'I'm not appreciated' and 'My kids are ungrateful for all the sacrifices I've made for them....If they only knew how hard I work for them, they might actually give me the recognition I deserve!'"

"They never help me."

"No one cares about all the things I do for this family."

"He always acts like this!"

"I will show this kid who is boss…!"

Never say never…or always.

Always and *never* have a habit of showing up. There are extremes that don't take into account all the great ways our families show us they care. We can fixate on that moment, look through that lens of emotion, and create stories that motivate our own bad behavior.

This is when we find ourselves on the train to crazy town.

Why does this happen?

There are so many reasons we think the things we think. We are meaning-making machines. Humans perceive a situation and immediately interpret what they see. Then they move into forming beliefs about these interpretations and choose into action.

Let's break that down a bit, starting with perception. Perception is what we see, right? It is what we observe around us. Almost immediately, we move from seeing the world around us to *interpreting* it, to making meaning.

We interpret situations through the lens of our own life experience and our conditioning. We want to organize the information we are taking in—and we do. Our views get shaped and molded over time, based on the experiences we have.

When we are in our logical mind, we can see the evidence that points to how amazing our family is and what a great job we do with parenting, and we feel good and we celebrate the wins. But when we are emotionally triggered, as we are when riding the emotional freight train, we forget our skills and our successes, and all we focus on negative moments.

There is a term for this—"negativity bias." It refers to the ways that negative experiences hold more weight with us, while positive, joyful experiences come and go without us hanging on to them. We can, again, thank our early ancestors for this tendency, because it is one of the ways we were able to make quick decisions and stay alive.

It does not, however, serve us on our parenting journey.

Where do the thoughts come from?

Often when we think we are responding to our children, we are actually responding to an old hurt, a wound from our life experience that hasn't healed.

At the start of high school, when she was 14, my daughter had an epic meltdown. She was crying and carrying on. This was bigger than any meltdown we had experienced with her so far. She told me she didn't want to live with our family anymore.

Whaaaaaaaaaaaat the fuck?

I lost my breath. My whole body went rigid. I didn't say anything. I wasn't present to her pain. I wasn't listening to her or to what she needed. Instead, I was in my own head, in my own hurt. My reaction really took me by surprise.

It was as if my whole body was wrapped in a tight blanket. I was unable to form words. I was stunned and lost in my head. Fear had totally taken over. The emotional freight train wasn't roaring along this time; it was more of a stunned realization that I had no idea what to do. I was in freeze mode.

When I was 14, I told *my* mom I wanted to move in with my father. This was a really painful time in my life, and that moment began a nearly 10-year estrangement between my mother and myself.

All the pain I felt during that time rushed back to me after my daughter said, "I don't want to live here."

If you have had experiences in your life that have been chaotic and that led to pain, being triggered emotionally years later can take you back to that place, or back to the emotion and the messages that you experienced during that time.

If you pay attention to how you respond to your kids and take a hard look at how you react at certain times, you might see that your response at a particular time wasn't really about your child, it was about the hurts of your past.

Why does any of this matter?

Have you ever been standing in front of your sink, full of rage, and tried to tell yourself to calm down? Have you ever been in the car with screaming kids in the back, trying to talk yourself out of lecture mode? Have you ever found yourself sitting on your bed, working on taking deep breaths, and trying to will yourself to get it together?

In those moments, has there ever been a voice inside you that says, "Screw it, I'm pissed and they all deserve to know"?

I know what it is like to try and talk yourself down. It's hard. But when we learn about our own physical response, we're more likely to be successful.

This is what I mean when I talk about getting curious and paying attention to our body. When we begin to notice that our body is experiencing tension, and we go inside with curiosity like, "Whoa! That response really flooded me with tension and anger. What is this moment triggering inside me?" we can get a clearer understanding of the **why** behind how we are responding.

And, when we begin to recognize where our response is coming from, we can get better at choosing to pause, choosing to take a breath, and choosing to stay in the present moment.

> *"As I built awareness of my own triggered reactions, it became clear to me that all the times it felt like my feelings were someone else's fault, it was really an opportunity for me to look inward and learn more about myself. Why does this behavior trigger me? What is it bringing up in me? If I could manage to become an observer of my experience rather than the miserable person having the experience, I was able to pause long enough to make a different choice."*
>
> *– Mama Lauren R.*

CHAPTER THREE

Who is Causing Your Derailment?

When we ride the emotional freight train, we typically don't ride it alone. We tend to bring along whoever is closest to us. That means our children or our partner.

Our past hurt, pain, and trauma ride with us on the train, as does a deep need for control.

That's what I mean when I say you are not the only one riding the train.

We don't live in a vacuum. We are emotional beings having emotional experiences, and raising other emotional beings who have limited life skills. Is it any wonder things get dicey?

There are so many entry points on the train. Choosing to parent with Joyful Courage requires that we learn to recognize when we are being swept up and away.

If your partner comes home in a bad mood, complaining about something that happened in their day, they might be short with you. How do you start to feel?

Your son won't stop complaining about his sister, the weather, and how he never gets to pick the TV show when the family sits down to watch something together. How do you start to feel?

Some of us are better at letting others' energy roll off us, and others are super sensitive about it. I'm going to guess the majority fall somewhere in the middle.

Again, this chapter is about learning to become ever more aware of what is happening in our experience, and perhaps discovering some places where we have been unconsciously allowing that outside energy to pull us onto the train.

Our children also have emotional freight trains.

For many of us, the emotional freight train experience began after we had children. Even then, perhaps it took a few years for us to really understand how deeply their behavior could affect us.

The fact of the matter is, children increase your stress level. Never before has so much of our self-worth been connected to someone else. Even when they're babies, we feel a sense of pride when we can say, "They sleep through the night" or "She took to breastfeeding right away."

When we dreaded others asking about how our children slept, fed, or took to potty training, it was typically because we were emotionally invested in how our child "performed." It could be painful to share the truth. Maybe they were up all night. Maybe they weren't able to latch or struggled with potty training.

And this isn't just an early years' phenomenon. As I've mentioned, while I was working on this book, my daughter was in her first year of high school. I had never been more confronted with my control and attachment issues than I was at that time. The train was always right there, it seemed, idling away with the doors open, waiting for that moment when I just couldn't take it anymore.

Why does this happen? We know in our heads that all children are individuals, that they move at their own pace, and that they need to make mistakes and experience the world so they can learn to navigate it. Yet we find that we tend to take on their behavior as our own personal failure.

When we aren't paying attention, our children can jump on their own emotional freight train and pull us along for the ride.

How fun is that?

As I mentioned early on, fear is a big piece of what gets in the way. I think another part of it is the idea of permanence—now that we are in whatever the current challenge is, we are here to stay. Forever.

It's that always-and-never mindset, right?

We think it's forever, and we brace ourselves.

When we do that, we find ourselves in a fighter's stance, either metaphorically or physically. When we are ready to fight, we assume there will be a winner and a loser, and I sure as hell am not going to be the loser.

It becomes a stand-off on the crazy train.

Not everyone does this. I am in awe of parents who seem to have mastered the art of surrendering. They're the parents who allow their children to make mistakes. They seem to really trust the process. They believe that all paths lead out of the forest. I look at them with envy, imagining that they have no fear for their children, that they have truly let go.

You know who I am talking about. The parent at the park who has a child that is falling apart, and they calmly rub their back and seem to have no tension at all in their face or body. They have that smile that isn't for the watchers' benefit, it is some inner knowing that this is all a part of life and everyone is going to be fine….

As I waded through the early months of my daughter going to high school, I was learning to let go while still setting boundaries for her. I was still fearful and I questioned my every move.

I was called into a new relationship with trust. It's a trust that's bigger, deeper, and more profound than simply saying, "I trust you." It requires me to acknowledge and hold space for my children to be on their journey, and to believe that we are all going to be okay.

While I had expected my teen to try on some risky behavior during her high school years, I did not expect everything to show up during her first year. They say that the risk-taking part of the teenage brain develops faster that the risk-assessment part. This was clearly the case with my daughter. The high school environment proved to be incredibly discouraging to her, and that sense of discouragement colored her decision making.

So, trust has become: I trust that you are going to learn from your mistakes.

Sounds simple enough, doesn't it? But here is the thing: if our kids are going to learn from their mistakes, then they have to make them (please point me toward the sand so I can put my head in it).

And our kids only learn from their mistakes when we stay out of the way. That means it isn't about disappointing us, or how angry we are, or what we are going to take away. We get out of the way and we engage them in conversation about their choices in a way that allows them to connect the dots between what they want most and what they want now.

I think there may be a book about parenting teens in my future....

Parenting with Joyful Courage means growing and expanding what we know to be true and being open to new ways of thinking.

When our past shows up on the train.

We might sometimes find that our past is a passenger keeping us on the train.

Our life experiences influence how we behave, how we respond, and how we see the world. We have been conditioned by the messages, both spoken and unspoken, by the adults in our life as we grew up. We learned to do what we needed to do to stay safe and connected.

Remember that I mentioned the work of Alfred Adler landing on human behavior being movement towards belonging and significance? From our earliest days, we are looking to connect, and to know that we matter. And we are making sense of the relationships and experiences that we have early in life.

In attachment science, it has been determined that babies develop trust in their caregivers and in themselves when their needs are met. When babies cry and they're fed, they learn to trust that those around them will take care of them. Those responses help to shape babies' overall sense of safety and trust in their world.

Parents are always doing the best they can with the tools they have.

Sometimes our well-intentioned parents left us with the perception that we weren't good enough as we were. In an effort to connect and have significance, we may have developed into overachievers or perfectionists, while also carrying the weight of low self-worth.

Or perhaps those well-intentioned parents didn't want to see us struggle. Maybe they always came to the rescue. They wanted to make us feel good and safe, but their "helicopter" parenting resulted in us having deficient coping skills, or perhaps entitlement, and/or perhaps a victim mentality. Looking through the lens of belonging, we may now feel connected and as though we matter only when others do things for us.

We all carry beliefs and ideas about the world based on our experiences.

What kept us safe and connected as children turns into our default operating system in adulthood. We all move through the world with the lens we developed in the first part of our lives. And sometimes this lens adds to the challenges we are having with our kids.

The exciting news is that we can always expand that lens. We can shift our perspective, and interrupt the thoughts and beliefs that keep us stuck. It just takes practice. And yes, I am going to help you with that.

Our need for control.

The final "passenger" that can show up on the emotional freight train is a need for control. Control is a slippery thing, isn't it? We can shift from feeling like we have it handled to feeling like having it "handled" is an illusion.

Parenting is fertile ground for discovering and addressing control issues.

My name is Casey, I am a controller.

Don't get me wrong, keeping the household together, managing the calendar, feeding the family, and doing all the rest of the things no one even realizes I do takes skill. It takes organization, systems, routines, attention, and forethought.

These are positive aspects of being "in control." But problems develop when I'm inflexible. It sends the message to the people around me that they aren't good enough, that they haven't done "it" right, and no one can do "it" as well as I can.

That mentality invites power struggles. It can also be something that really breaks our relationship with our children. They decide they don't want to help because, I mean, why bother? Or they drag their feet, or they become slow, distracted, or simply ignore us.

Then, of course, we react to that behavior. We react to the power struggles, to the feet dragging, to the "selective" listening—often without recognizing that it is actually our rigidity that is the main source of the problem, and not our children.

Here are a few stories from the Joyful Courage community:

"A few months ago, I flipped my lid when my six-year-old daughter wouldn't let me brush her hair in the morning. In the moment, it felt very important that she not leave the house with her hair a mess. I shamed her, blamed her, and ultimately forced her to let me brush her hair. Not my best moment."

– Mama Lauren R.

"My daughter is intelligent and her handwriting is often illegible, which drives me crazy. Part of me has this need to control how she presents her work so that her intelligence is seen, but it stems from my childhood issues as well. She had an assignment in second grade which I made her do over again. The teacher emailed me that I didn't need to put pressure on her regarding her handwriting

at such a young age. The concepts were more important than the writing. I still need to work on that piece."

– Mama Ana P.

"I tend to hold onto control about something needing to get done now. Clean that up, brush your teeth, move it..."

– Mama Liz N.

So, what next?

We don't have much perspective when we are on the emotional freight train. It exists but we don't have access to it. The emotional freight train is all about us. We are the star. Everyone else is to blame when we are on that train.

To parent with Joyful Courage—to use those opportunities to grow into an ever more evolved, present, connected human being—it's important to explore the landscape of where you are.

Remember, Joyful Courage is parenting on purpose. And parenting on purpose can only happen when we expand our awareness of what is happening in the present moment.

PART
TWO

How to Get Off the Emotional Freight Train

Gah! Okay! We find ourselves on the train—and it's normal to find ourselves there. But as we become more able to *notice* the train, we'll begin to realize that we can choose to get off!

But it can be challenging to shift in the heat of the moment. It's hard to talk ourselves out of our feelings. It can feel good—sad to say—to make other people feel as bad as we feel in the moment.

But when the freight train fades into the distance, we are left to clean up our mess.

This section of the book will help you figure out what to do when you see that emotional freight train coming down the track towards you.

At the end of the day, it is up to *you*. It means digging deep and recognizing that Joyful Courage already exists inside of you, and then learning how to access it.

CHAPTER FOUR

Where Would You Rather This Train Be Going?

How many of us have mapped out how we *want* to respond to challenging situations?

We tend to be clear about what we *don't* want. We don't want to yell, we don't want to blame and shame, and we don't want to be so angry.

I invite you to consider who you *want* to be as a parent when things are going well *and* when the shit hits the fan.

How do you want to show up when…?

- *Your son hits his little sister?*

- *Your daughter tells you she hates you?*

- *Yet again no one has cleaned up after themselves?*

- *Your teenager lets you know that you don't know anything?*

- *Your toddler slaps you in the face?*

- *Your son hides under the covers and won't get up for school…every day?*

- *The kids are whining about the food you serve?*

- *You find out your child is experimenting with drugs?*

How do you want to be when your child is having an emotional breakdown?

When I think about this, and coach parents around this, I invite them to consider their *intention*, their *desired way of being*. We don't want to be scary or mean. We don't want to intimidate, threaten, or bribe our kids, especially when we realize those are short term solutions. We don't want to *freak out...*

But what *do* we want? When we take all those things away, what do we actually have left?

Finding our intention.

I use the word "intention" because when we *know* how we want to be, we are one step closer to being it.

If we don't spend time exploring and practicing *how we do want to show up*, we'll revert back to the way we've always done things.

Wait a minute, you may be thinking, *why am I spending time thinking about* me *when* my kid *is the problem?*

The answer is simple: your biggest problem is you, not them.

I will just give you a moment to let that sink in.

Joyful Courage parents know that their ability to influence their children lies in the relationship they are able to build with their children. We shape that relationship by the way we show up.

Let's go back a bit here.

Remember at the beginning of the book when I mentioned that I am a Positive Discipline Trainer? And that Positive Discipline is all about creating a sense of *belonging and significance.*

What the hell does that mean?

What humans want most, what we need most, what supports us in thriving, is a sense of connection (belonging) and knowing that we matter (significance). This is true for **all** humans—kids and grownups both.

Think about it. How do you show up in a group when it is a bunch of people who you feel totally solid with? People, friends, and family, who you know love you for being you and appreciate what you do? My guess is that you show up as authentic, that you let your voice and your ideas be heard. This is your happy place and it shows!

Now, what about when you are in a group of strangers, or people that you don't really connect with, but you know each other on a surface level? Do you bring your whole self? Do you share your deepest thoughts and beliefs? What about when the group begins to make decisions on your behalf that you don't like?

We all do better when we feel seen and heard, and connected, and when we feel that we have some influence over our lives. We just do. And this is as important for *our kids* as it is for us parents.

Back-to-school backlash.

In 2013, we had a really great summer. We were busy with camps and sunny days in the neighborhood, and I felt like we were in the sweet spot.

Back-to-school time rolled around, and I was ready for the school year to begin. I love schedules and structures and routines, and I knew just how to transition my kids into the school year. I had a clear vision of what it would look like, and I had no doubt that my kids would fall in line.

I knew it would be important for the kids to have a set routine when they got home from school, and I figured last year's routine would be fine. For my then eight-year-old son, Ian, I added a 15-minute reading session, and I decided that would also be when he made his lunch for the next day so we didn't have to hassle with him after dinner.

I asked Ian which day he would like to work on his new after-school routine, and he picked Monday. When Monday rolled around, I asked him to list off what he needed to do after school. He told me, and I wrote it down, adding the two new items to the list, and then gave it to him to copy in his own handwriting.

If it is in his handwriting, doesn't that translate to buy-in? Time would tell.

For me, an after-school routine means my kids *know* what needs to be done and they do it. Easy-peasy. I tend to think they *want* to just cruise though their tasks.

It turns out my son had different ideas. Here he was, an almost eight-year-old boy who had just gotten off the bus after spending seven hours away from home. He had spent all day following directions and doing the right thing, and when he got home, he just wanted to eat and relax.

The routine chart we created was a mess. Ian wandered around the house, taking *forever* to do the simplest task. He wouldn't acknowledge I'd spoken to him, and it sent me into a crazy spin cycle. *He thinks he doesn't have to do anything and I won't do anything about it!*

He doesn't care at all about what others do for him!

He's so entitled!

He thinks he can just act however he wants.

He's hitting the preadolescent boy stage—he hates me!

Oh no!

I was *totally* on the emotional freight train.

It got ugly. He pushed against this new reality, full of structure and routines, and I fell into fear. I pushed back, overwhelmed, and I grasped for control of the situation.

I thought I was still using my tools. I thought I was engaging him with curiosity. I thought I was inviting cooperation and contribution.

When I asked him, *"What do we do with our dishes after we eat?"* I scrunched up my forehead and used an incredulous tone. The question really sounded like, *"Are you an idiot?"*

I could have just said, *"Please join me on the train."*

The next Friday, the whole family was drawing at the counter together. My son got frustrated with how his drawing looked and he fell apart. Big time. He lost it. My husband tried to give him suggestions on how to fix his drawing, and then he encouraged him to start again. I added my thoughts and suggestions, and his meltdown took on new energy.

"You are always telling me what to do!" he shouted at me,

Ugh. Dagger to my heart.

He was right. Summer ended, school started, and I went into full dictator mode. *Have I mentioned my controlling tendencies?* I'm working on this, but it still sneaks up on me.

"You are always telling me what to do."

It was humbling to hear. My little boy had had enough, and he was able to tell me how I had hurt him. It made me feel both proud and ashamed.

Once he calmed down, I got really close to him and gathered his little, big boy body in my arms and let him know how much I loved him. I told him I was sorry for how I had treated him. I told him I would be different.

The next day, I worked really hard to check in with him. I asked what he thought about things. I didn't assume I knew best. I was curious about what he thought. I caught myself when I wanted to make assumptions or suggestions, and instead I gave him space and time to ask for help. I worked on connecting with him.

It's a tricky dance. Sometimes I start to think that if I am not continuously reminding (read: nagging) him about what he needs to do, he just won't do it.

When I stopped having faith in my son, he lived up to those expectations.

Hmm, isn't that interesting? What happened to encouragement? What happened to connection? What happened to getting into my child's world?

A few nights later, I called my son into the living room to talk about his apparent lack of desire to contribute. I told him I felt frustrated and angry because it seemed like he thought he could do whatever he wanted. I told him I didn't *really* know if that's what he was thinking. I told him I wanted to know.

I opened the door.

My son shared a lot with me that night. He told me that when school started, it felt like everything was different and it was hard for him to adjust. I shared that I felt like *he* was different. He told me *I* seemed to act different.

I told him I wanted to be better. I told him I wanted to be helpful, and I trusted he could be helpful too. We talked about how we both had responsibilities. We talked about how if one of us didn't' follow through with those responsibilities, it would be hard for both of us. Ian said he wanted to move his reading time to just before bed, and together we decided on 7:30 p.m. He also wanted me to help him make his lunch. I told him I would be happy to help.

I also told him there might be times when I was busy, and he might have to make lunch without me. I told him I knew he could do it.

Big sigh.

It was messy, but I left feeling hopeful.

I was grateful to my son for teaching me how easy it is to get off track, to get on the emotional freight train without realizing it. I am grateful that my son knows enough about how he wants to be treated to be able to engage in a conversation about it—even if it showed up after a meltdown.

Misbehavior as code for discouragement.

I share that story because it's *useful* to know that when grownups feel disconnected, underappreciated, or ignored, we can fall into behavior that is hurtful rather than helpful.

When our kids feel disconnected, underappreciated, or ignored, they can fall into the same behavior.

What happens, particularly with kids and their developing brains, is that when they are feeling that disconnection or lack of influence, they go into fight-or-flight mode. From that place, kids mistake controlling, bossing, whining, and/or hurting as ways to feel belonging and significance.

Ian gave me all sorts of information about what he wanted. He just delivered it in a way that caught me off guard. I couldn't hear what he needed because I was trapped in my own experience.

This is totally true for adults too. Consider the last time you snapped at your partner. Perhaps he didn't do his dishes or left his socks on the floor (again).

When we feel *connected* inside that relationship, we tend to respond from a lighthearted, loving place.

When we *don't* feel connected, we don't say, *"Hey, I'm feeling really disconnected, and your socks on the floor are making it worse—can I have a hug?"* No. We snap. We jump on the emotional freight train, and we go down the tracks of pain and more disconnection.

Who do you want to be?

Back to intention.

Deciding how you will show up becomes a proactive, helpful tool in being a more present, connected, positive, and conscious parent. This is Joyful Courage! This starts the ripple effect. It can influence the behavior of the people around you.

It's the difference between *responding* and *reacting*.

When you think about the most challenging situations in your life, consider what they call for. Patience? Calm? Presence? Grace? Kindness? Love?

Does the situation call for Playfulness? Surrender? Humor?

Playfulness and letting go are both big ones for me. Kids love to play. They learn through play. And when we can be playful with our requests and responses, we all feel better. However, playful is not my go-to way of being. I tend to be serious and controlling with the kids. This is not useful; it shakes my children's perception of influence.

Therefore, it actually *serves me* to breathe in some playfulness when I know I am going to talk with my kids about a chore they haven't completed, for example.

As my children moved into middle and high school, I noticed I was also being called into practicing *trust*, which I have written about already. The character of Reverend Shaw Moore says it best in one of my favorite scenes of the movie *Footloose*: "If we don't start trusting our children, how will they become trustworthy?"

It is up to us to grow our awareness and be willing to practice new ways of showing up for our children, even when it is hard to do. Try some new ways of showing up —practice them, play with them, make them your own.

This isn't just thinking *"I will be more playful with the kids,"* or *"I am going to be better at trusting my daughter."* It's bringing playfulness and trust into your way of being in the world. It's bigger than just a concept.

CHAPTER FIVE

What You Need to Know to Slow the Train Down

As I write this, I am working on changing some habits that have been a part of who I am for as long as I can remember. I am a fixer. I am an opinion giver. I believe that I see the world so clearly, and that others simply have to see what I see to come to their own understanding of their situation.

It's so obnoxious!

And it has become a part of my wiring. I launch into what I think quicker than I sometimes realize I am doing it.

This is not helpful when raising teenagers.

And more often than not, this is when my teenagers shut down, turn away, and close the door to relationships. And of course, when they do this, all of my approval baggage is triggered, and I get bent out of shape and respond from a place of hurt and fear.

Do you see how this is a challenge that I directly contribute to?

My goal is to be in a solid relationship with my kids. To be a sounding board, a safe landing, a nonjudgmental, healthy adult—one with whom they feel seen, understood, and accepted by.

When I take a look at the dynamic that I am creating from the outside, I see how my fix-it, advice-giving tendency is challenging to my teenagers. From their perspective, I don't hear them out, I don't understand, I don't trust them, or treat them as capable human beings.

Okay, but aren't we supposed to offer advice? Aren't we supposed to guide our children and let them know what we think??

Well, yes, *and* people can listen better when they feel that they are also listened to.

So, I have begun to ask permission to give my opinion. I ask, "Do you want to know what I think?" or "Can I offer something?" and let my kids decide if they want to hear from me or not.

When I launch into one of my "Just listen to me, I know everything" moments, I am learning to catch myself and own it, "Wow, I bet that didn't feel very respectful," or "You didn't ask for my opinion—I just gave it. Sorry about that."

We always have the opportunity to turn things around, to recognize when we are headed to the train station, and to make the choice to pause and take a different route.

We can always slow things down. There is always a choice. We have so much power when it comes to designing our experience.

I want to invite you to claim space; I want to invite you to see that there is always an opportunity to claim the experience you are having, to take an active role, and to influence what's happening so you get closer to what you want most.

When we allow the train to pick us up, we are on autopilot. We allow our emotions to take control, then more often than not, when the ride is over, we aren't happy with the route we took.

Claiming your space at the station is choosing Joyful Courage. It's choosing to see what's happening and deciding you will navigate the experience.

In this chapter, you'll learn how to recognize where you are, grow your awareness, and create space and time to be the parent you want to be.

The Pause.

Remember I mentioned earlier that there are some parents who have been through my workshops and then come to me and say, "Casey, I really want to use the tools you talk about during your parenting classes, but I find that I get triggered, and then I act out of anger before I realize what I am doing!"

This is a common experience. We feel as though the switch goes off and our anger takes control. But we can work to change this....

There is a pause that exists between the action and your reaction. Back in Chapter Two, I encouraged you to explore what your body feels like when you're on the emotional freight train. This is important! Our bodies can tell us when the train is pulling into the station.

Becoming more aware of what's happening in our bodies as it happens helps create the pause we need to be more thoughtful and courageous regarding how we show up for our children. This is where we find our Joyful Courage.

Think about being triggered. It is a terrible experience. It's tight, hot, and rigid. It's difficult to stop that angry energy. This is why we snap! This is why we lash out.

There were times at the dinner table when my teenager just could not deal with the rest of us. We ate too loud! God forbid that we tried to talk to her! She wouldn't make eye contact with any of us. She spoke in one-word answers, which often translated into the unspoken message of "I hate every one of you."

It killed me.

Killed me.

My physical response to this was immediate. I tensed up, I clenched my jaw, my eyes narrowed, my breath got shallow...I was ready for the fight!

The train has arrived!

Sometimes that train pulled up and I would hop right on. I leaned into her and I let her know what I thought about how she is acting. I met mean with mean. Typically, one of us would leave the table in a huff.

The Joyful Courage process is simple but it's not easy. It takes practice. I am still in the practice stage myself.

> *"My toddler got hold of a black permanent marker. I had talked with my husband and daughter multiple times to please be aware of the things left out where the baby could get hold of them. This included markers and paint, which he both found and used. I was at the grocery store and my husband was home with the kids. When I came home, our new couch was covered in marker. So was our son, and the hardwood floor. I lost it. LOST IT! I was so angry, not just because of the marks, but because I felt unheard, insignificant, and completely resentful. Plus, I always seemed to*

be the one to clean up all the messes. I was screaming and crying, and I wished a spaceship would just swoop out of the floor and take me to outer space."

– Mama Ana P.

"One time my two youngest children wanted to play a board game with me. At first, they agreed on which game to play—Race to the Treasure—but then my son noticed a Paw Patrol game he wanted to play. They each grabbed their board game while arguing about which game we would all play. I could feel the emotional freight train coming...I was getting annoyed (we only had time for one game). I tried to encourage them to come to an agreement regarding which game we would play but neither of them would budge. They each began to dump the contents of their boxes out onto the carpet of the playroom, still arguing. The emotional freight train arrived and I jumped on board. I felt my body get tense, and I started to feel really angry, and I just started yelling at them. I shouted that we did not have time to play two games, that they had made a big mess, and that they needed to choose which game we were playing or we would not be playing anything. Oh, and that they needed to clean up the mess. I'm sure I yelled that too. And of course, after I was done with riding the freight train, I felt awful for having yelled at my two young little kiddos who just needed a bit more help making a choice...."

– Mama Tricia W.

"One time in the car, my daughter blamed me for being late to pick her up. Her dance school had let out 30 minutes early from one location in order to switch to another location, and I was one of only a few parents who didn't stay and had gone shopping. I pulled up four minutes late (she had then been waiting 34 minutes), and I apologized to her for being the last one there, and I expressed that I understood her upset. But she couldn't let it go. I empathized with how hard it is to be the last student picked up, and I then explained I couldn't have predicted that they would get out early. I knew she was frustrated with them and taking it out on me. Then she turned it to, "You never do anything for me." Whoa! The freight train pulled in for me to jump on board. My whole body filled with adrenaline, and the steam felt like it was coming out of my ears—the fight reflex coursing through me. It was an instinctive defense mechanism, and afterwards I could say that I know this pattern well, but in the moment, I went to crazy town. Screaming and even cursing at my child about all that I do for her—such as right this minute driving her from one dance location to another. Then she went to an anxious place and I could immediately see that I had overreacted."

– Mama Liz N.

Oh, the discomfort!

But take a deep breath and try to find the pause within that discomfort.

When we begin to feel the discomfort; it can overpower us, and it can lead to us jumping right on to the freight train. But if we can just take a couple of breaths, if we can just find the pause, this is where we can access Joyful Courage. This is where we can choose between slipping into autopilot or being conscious of what is happening internally for us. The initial physical reaction doesn't last forever. When we are willing to feel it, let it run its course, and acknowledge and accept what's happening, we can get to the other side.

When we can sit with the discomfort for a while and do nothing, we give ourselves (and our children) *the gift of thoughtful response.*

This is not about stuffing our feelings away or denying our anger. This is about being brave enough to *be* with those feelings. This is about developing resilience and endurance. It's about reminding ourselves that we're going to be okay.

This is the *pause* that we need in order to make a more thoughtful choice. Maybe we've been skipping over it to sidestep our discomfort.

That dinnertime angst? It didn't always send me down the tracks. Sometimes I would sit with how I felt. The rejection, the hurt, the anger. I would sit with thoughts like: *She has no idea how good she has it, what a brat, I'll show her.* I would have these thoughts and then slowly they would go to: *she is having a hard time, she is unhappy, I am curious about what is going on in her life....*

When I would do this, we would get through dinner and our relationship remained intact. When I let the experience pass through me, I could connect with her later and have a helpful conversation about her behavior. When I stayed present, more often than not *she* would make amends for how she acted at the table.

Here is some of what others have said about *growing the pause* and practicing being present in the moment:

> *"As I built awareness of my own triggered reactions, it became clear to me that all the times it felt like my feelings were someone else's fault, it was really an opportunity for me to look inward*

and learn more about myself. Why does this behavior trigger me? What is it bringing up for me? If I could manage to become an observer of my experience rather than the miserable person having the experience, I was able to pause long enough to make a different choice."

– Mama Lauren R.

"As I have learned to become a purposeful observer when I am triggered, I have discovered that I was really missing me. I was not caring for myself and I had no support system. I had not created boundaries around time for my jobs that the children could not participate in (like paying the bills, or coordinating doctor appointments or therapists, or emailing teachers about their behavior concerns); and nor had I created space for me to nurture myself and my own interests outside of my children and my husband. There was nothing left for me to give beyond maintaining the routine. I could not show up in a way that reflected who I think I am, which further enforced the voice echoing 'I am not good enough' in my head."

– Mama Nelly B.

"I was really missing how attached I was to old stories and hurt. Even though the behavior was different, those old feelings of being dismissed and unseen would come flooding back with massive force, at times with a stronger energy than the original experience. I was

lacking the awareness that my children's behavior wasn't about me, that their experience wasn't tied to my old hurts."

– Mama Monica Z.

Say yes!

As a Joyful Courage parent, I invite you to rejoice in the opportunity to *grow*. Make space for your feelings. Trust you can handle them. Be willing to *feel* your experience.

This is what it looks like to claim your space at the station. This is finding the pause.

Then what?

Where are our feet in the present moment?

As I alluded to in the previous section, all of this work has a lot to do with recognizing what is alive in the present moment. When we get swept up onto the emotional freight train, we can feel disconnected from our body; we can get trapped in our heads.

What is something that can anchor us to the here and now? *Our feet.*

Our feet are always present in the moment. One tool for grounding into the practice of staying present and aware, no matter what our children are doing, is to feel our feet on the ground. We want to feel our feet on the ground and stay *rooted* in our vision of who we want to be for our children.

Getting into the practice of noticing your experience, and rooting into your feet, gives a *physical* connection to a mental and emotional situation. As my mentor and friend, Krista Petty Raimer, master coach and facilitator, and founder of *Boldly Embody Life*, says, "Our *feet* are never in the future or the past; they are always in the present."

Beginning our practice of being present with simply "feeling our feet" gives us a starting point, a stepping stone, and a small move to shift our experience.

Here is how I use this tool....

My children share a lot with me.

Like, *a lot*.

Typically, when they have something really big to tell me, they say, *"Mom? I need to tell you something."*

Whenever I hear those words, I immediately think: *find my feet.*

I do this because I want to stay present no matter what they tell me. I want to be available, curious, and nonjudgmental. I want to be able to choose Joyful Courage. I want to rejoice *in the opportunity they give me to practice being my best self.*

Because I never know what might follow after I say, *"What is it?"*

As my kids get older, it gets more important for me to *hear* them, to *see* them, and to *listen deeply* to them as they share the experiences they are going through, *without* my being clouded by fear, launching into advice, or being taken away on the emotional freight train.

Kids need us to be grounded. They need us to be curious and open. They need to know, *really know*, we are going to love them no matter what. They need to know we can handle whatever it is that they are struggling with.

Otherwise, they simply won't share. They won't come to us, and that's when things get scary.

Let your body take the lead.

You'll find that it is incredibly difficult to talk your *mind* into a new way of being. It really does start with the *body*. Letting our body lead allows us to bypass the barriers that exist in our mind, to move towards the way of being that serves us.

Have you ever tried to talk yourself out of being triggered? Have you ever tried to convince yourself to jump off that runaway train? It's tough. We are masters at justifying why we feel how we feel and to pass around blame.

The *body* is a different access point for change. Instead of depending on our mind to let go of the trigger, we can take action with our body. We can access our breath, we can slow our heart, we can pull back our shoulders. We can stay present.

Claim your space. Find your pause. Feel your feet on the ground. It's about being alert and conscious of what you're experiencing. It's about having the perspective to see beyond *your* emotions so you can see what your child needs.

You don't actually have to make those split-second decisions in a split second. There is time to find the present moment, time to connect with what is happening for you, and time to expand your perspective.

CHAPTER SIX

Pulling the Switch
to Your Destination

In the last chapter we played with what happens when we decide to take ownership of our actions. You heard from some members of the Joyful Courage community about what happened for them when they reflected on their experience.

If you feel like you're ready to try some reflection, use the following questions as journal prompts to help guide you.

What is happening for me right now?

What is my body telling me?

What is it that I am trying to control?

How can I help myself in this moment?

What do I need?

This chapter is all about engaging in a practice that will support you in shifting your experience when you do find yourself on the emotional freight train. As you grow in this practice, you will develop your own intuition and wisdom. And you will find that your relationships with your children will strengthen as well.

The practice we are going to dig into is something that you can do anytime, anywhere. It is available for any situation, no matter how big or small. It is a practice that will always work for you, moving you in the direction you want to go.

I call it the Three Bs: Breath. Body. Balcony.

Your Breath.

I know you are reading this book to help yourself show up differently for your family. I know you are looking for tools that can support you. The good news is that the first part of the Three Bs is something that is working for you *all* the time, whether you are thinking about it or not.

Our breath.

Breathing is an automatic function of the brain, along with blinking, our heart beating, swallowing, and digestion. Your brain controls these functions without you thinking about them.

When you inhale, you make your heart beat faster. When you exhale, you send a signal to your heart that it can slow down. A fast heartbeat is often associated with a stimulated nervous system. When we talk about parenting, there are loads of situations and experiences that can stimulate our nervous system. When we become emotionally overwhelmed, or triggered by someone in our life, our heartbeat speeds up. We go into fight-or-flight mode.

When you pay attention to your breath, when you feel the sensation of the air entering and exiting your body, when you consciously lengthen your exhales, you can move from overwhelm to calm.

When you are calm and connected, you can choose Joyful Courage.

"The space between my trigger and how I respond is...always available. We always have a choice. I acknowledge myself, feel my feet on the ground, adjust my shoulders, and take a breath. A mantra is also helpful, such as 'I can do hard things.'"

– Mama Heidi B.

"When I'm triggered, I have trained myself to pause and take a deep breath. I usually close my eyes and 'go inward' for a moment. I have a little conversation with myself, usually repeating a mantra and thinking about how I'm going to respond. My eight-year-old son calls the voice we each have inside our heads our 'inner guidance counselor' who helps us decide what to do."

– Mama Lauren R.

"When I feel triggered, I inhale slowly through my nose, and I try to focus on the sensation of the air sweeping through my nostrils. I then exhale slowly through my mouth, and try to release any air that's left in my lungs. I use a short mantra to change my self-talk; I might say something along the lines of, 'This is temporary, I am capable. They are small. We are all learning' or 'We can get through this.'"

– Mama Monica Z.

Want to practice?

- Start by bringing your attention to your breath.

- Feel it move in and out of your body.

- Hear the sound that your inhale and exhale make.

- Taste the flavor of your breath.

- See the way your body moves in the giving and receiving of air.

- Become present to the smells that you notice when being attentive to your breath.

- Enjoy 10 breaths in this place.

How do you feel? What do you notice about the quality of your breathing? What happened to your emotions and thoughts? What was your body invited to do?

Take some time to reflect on this experience. Find this guided breath exercise on my website: www.joyfulcourage.com/eftbook

Paying attention to your breathing lowers your stress and brings your nervous system toward a state of calm. Breath is a legit tool for this parenting journey, and a powerful tool to help you stay off the emotional freight train.

"Breath as a tool helps me to get grounded. When I practice noticing my breath throughout the day, it brings me back into the present moment. Mindful breathing takes me away from the swirling to-do list in my mind that can otherwise increase my general stress to a point that makes me more reactive."

— Mama Christie P.

"Breath is self-compassion. Breath is grounding. Breath is accepting that I am an imperfect human, and that is okay because I am having a hard time too."

— Mama Nelly B.

"Breath as a tool helps me to feel all of my body again in an instant. If I take a really deep breath, I can visualize the air going all the way down to my toes and up to my brain—it really helps me feel grounded again."

— Mama Tricia W.

The oldest part of our brain, the brainstem, has been a part of the human experience since the beginning. We are wired to respond to threats. (www.joyfulcourage.com/eftbook)

When we become triggered, and our brain stem kicks into gear, our nervous system takes over and keeps us in fight-or-flight mode. Our bodies want to keep us safe, but, again, our bodies can't always tell the difference between a threat that is a real threat to our safety and a child that is falling apart in front of us.

In these moments, one of the ways that we can shift from that emotional flooding to accessing Joyful Courage is to use our breath.

We can let go of the idea that we need to talk ourselves out of how we're feeling. We don't need to do that! We don't have to feel or think any certain way. All we need to do is recognize that we are triggered, recognize that we are about to step on that emotional freight train, and then bring our attention to our breath.

Just be there. Just focus on breathing.

Body.

Okay, so here we are with our breath. Great. What do we do now?

Once we choose to focus simply on breathing, our breath becomes an entry point into our bodies.

Our breath slows things down enough so we can notice what is happening on the inside. Where is there tension? What is happening with our shoulders and our jaw? What direction are we leaning?

"My muscles get tense, my heart rate increases, I can almost hear it accelerate at times now. My stomach drops, opens like a bottomless pit, or holds onto a dense ball. My jaw tightens and I bite my tongue. My body aches and wants to release all the energy it is generating and holding. I didn't realize I was holding on so tightly before this practice."

– Mama Nelly B.

"The way my body responds is that I get tight in my shoulder area and my jaw gets clenched. I also feel hot."

– Mama Amber F.

Here's what happens to me:

My jaw clenches, my shoulders go up and in, I lean forward, my eyes narrow, my face is super tight. I am ready for attack.

Then when I use my breath, I can meet my body where it is at. I become aware of my breath and pay attention to what's happening with my body.

I loosen my jaw, unclench my hands (did I mention the fists?), and I pull my shoulders back and down. I release the muscles in my face. I keep breathing and I adjust my posture. I keep breathing and I change the way I hold my body.

I release the tension. I release the feeling of urgency. I drop into the present moment. I find my feet.

This is where lightness and playfulness becomes available to me. This is where I can access trust and choose to let go. My breath brings me to my body awareness, and then, instead of reacting to my experience, *I am in charge of it.*

Try it with me right now. Allow your breath to take you into deeper awareness of your body. Where is there tension? Where are you clenching? What happens when you allow your breath to release those places in your body?

Think about what you want to bring to your relationships. Maybe that's connection, love, and kindness. When you are present in the moment, in a body that is relaxed and free of rigidity, you are more likely to feel as though you can access connection, love, and kindness.

This is for you, no one else. Play with this practice and when it helps you to become a more connected, loving, joyfully, courageous parent, share it with the world.

We spend so much time in our head. We worry about the future or feel guilty and regret the past. Sometimes we forget the most powerful place to be is in the moment. While our heads have the luxury to time travel, our bodies don't. So, let's start to use our bodies as a tool to help our minds be in the moment too.

Taking the balcony seat.

Okay, on to the final B, the balcony seat.

Have you ever had the experience where you are looking for a way to solve a problem and you just can't seem to come up with anything that works? You are pulling your hair out, feeling so spent and frustrated, and then someone walks in the room and says, "Oh hey, try this" and it is the *perfect* solution?

It's like when our friends talk to us about challenges they have with their kids. Do you ever find yourself giving them amazing advice, only to think: *damn, that would come in handy for me too!*

Well this process of using our breath to drop into our body actually helps us to take the outside observer view, or what I call the "balcony seat."

Coming into the present moment gives us space to take a few steps away from the challenge at hand. It gives us a broader view of the situation.

Picture this: You are at the grocery store with your young child *(I know, already feeling the stress),* and you are trying to move fast so that you can get home and make a meal for the family. You think you are in the clear, only a few more things on the list, and your child asks for a cookie.

"No, we are going to go home and make dinner," you say, super reasonably.

But that is all it takes—your child falls apart. And *you* try to keep it together. Does this sound familiar?

This is where we get hooked, right? This is where our blood starts to boil, our body gets tense, and we begin to think things like: *Oh my gosh, I have ruined this child. They think they can get away with anything. Spoiled little fill-in-the-blank. I can't give in.*

This is where the train pulls up. But you have a new practice. You have something you are going to try....

Take a deep breath. Take another deep breath, and really pay attention to how it feels to bring it into your body. Notice where you're tense and relax those areas. Pull your shoulders back, release your jaw, and feel your feet on the floor.

Imagine you can lift up and out of your situation and see it from an elevated point of view. This is *the balcony seat.*

From up here, you can see that your child is hungry. You can see that a trip to the grocery store straight after daycare, before your child had a snack, may have been too much to ask. You could say to yourself: *is there something I could grab right now for my child as a snack to help him get through the next 10 minutes at the grocery store?*

Taking the balcony seat is powerful.

"A time when I was able to take the balcony seat and see what was really going on with my child was when my eldest son was demanding snack after snack one day after school. I was able to recognize that he just couldn't be as hungry as he was proclaiming and whining on about—that something else must be going on. So, I switched gears and replied, 'I hear you really want a snack and at the same time we are done eating snacks right now.'

He was livid and he dropped to the kitchen floor, and thrashed around and shouted at me. I remained calm and I empathized with him that he was mad there were no more snacks available right now. He continued flailing about, kicking the cabinet doors, and he attempted to throw the plastic step stool that we keep in the kitchen. I intervened and said, 'It's okay to be mad, but we don't hit or throw things.' Then I switched back to saying, 'I'm here and you're safe.'

This went on for around seven to 10 minutes. It felt like his big emotions held him for an eternity. But I did not have an emotional freight train of my own to contend with right then. I had the view that he was riding his own emotional freight train, and I just wanted him to know he was safe and I was there for him.

In the end, he shouted at me about his rough day at school and the kids who had hit him. I was able to get closer to him and hug him, with his permission, as the train slowed down, and I spoke with him about this upsetting news.

That day I was so grateful I was able to take the balcony seat and support my son through his big emotions. He had experienced a very rough and scary day, and did not know how to express it to me. I am so grateful I was able to be present and there for him, to be gifted with his trust regarding the scary experience he had had that day—and to be allowed by him to get close enough with him so he felt he could share and know I was there to help."

— Mama Tricia W.

Regardless of what you decide to do, after you use this practice of "breath, body, balcony," you take your child's behavior less personally. You will be more available to them and able to see what they need in the moment. You will be better at staying off the crazy train.

But Casey, you may be thinking, *shouldn't our kids be able to handle a visit to the grocery store and behave in public? And be scolded for lashing out?*

Yes, of course! This isn't about catering to them; this isn't about being permissive or being at their beck and call. This is about being aware of what is *actually* happening instead of being reactive. It's about responding in a way that's helpful to ourselves and our children.

When we use this practice, we are able to see the bigger picture. When we use these tools, we can continue to nurture our relationship with our children. When we use this practice, we can be the parents we want to be.

The iceberg metaphor.

Think about your own behavior when you're short or rude, or just not your best.

What are some of the things that take you there? Is it when you are hungry? Tired? What about when you feel disrespected? What about when you feel disconnected, or as if the things you do don't matter to other people? What about when you feel discouraged?

All of these things get in the way of our best behavior. The same is true for kids.

When we can use our breath, body, and balcony seat, we can recognize that the behavior we see is only the tip of the iceberg. Then we are more able to respond to what's really going on under the surface.

So, going back to that example of the grocery store—our child may be hungry, our child may be tired, our child may not feel connected, our child perhaps hasn't been *included* in the grocery store trip.

When we acknowledge our children's needs, we set ourselves and our children up for success. We are better able to connect with them, they feel seen, and we've increased the likelihood that they'll be cooperative.

Again, this requires us to be in the present moment and to hold space for their experience. It also requires *us* to stay off the emotional freight train.

Breath, body, balcony.

Easier said than done, yes.

And it takes practice. Practice, practice, practice.

PART
THREE

Staying Off the
Emotional Freight Train

You know how if you go to a popular hiking trail, it is worn down and easy to follow? It's so easy that you can have a conversation with your hiking partner, look at the trees and plants around you, take in the beauty, and let your thoughts wander.

It's nice, right? You don't have to think too much about each step.

While hiking, have you ever looked around and noticed the game trails? The barely there indents in the forest that indicate where animals have been?

If you've ever tried to walk the game trail, you know it's tricky. You have to watch each step carefully and think about where you put your feet. It becomes challenging to talk to your friend or look around at the scenery. You might even trip a couple of times. Perhaps stumble and fall. You might even need a machete to clear the way.

But every time you walked that game trail, you would wear it down. You make it easier to follow. The more often you chose this path, the more familiar it would become.

And, when you stop using the old path, it grows over and becomes part of the forest.

When we try to learn something new, it's a lot like wearing down the game trail. Only we are creating a new pathway in our brain.

At first, it is really tricky. You're drawn back to the familiar way. It will feel like hard work to find your breath in the moment, to let go and be with your emotions.

It is frustrating work. It takes practice.

That's what this final section is all about: Creating a practice that will help you *notice* the train as it pulls into the station, and help you *choose* to do something different, to choose a *different* path than the one that is worn down and familiar. This next section is about taking personal responsibility for how you parent. It is about creating a practice to make this work *sustainable*.

CHAPTER SEVEN

Be Willing to Let the Train Go By

As I have mentioned throughout this book, a particularly challenging era with my daughter was when she was transitioning into high school. Both of us were taken by surprise by how intense it was. After a couple of really hard weeks, I took her out for coffee after school one day and I asked her what was going on.

I listened.

What she finally said to me was, "You and Daddy and Ian, you're all so *happy*. And you, you are just so *perfect*!" as tears ran down her face.

I was shocked to hear that this was her perspective, and I told her so.

"I told you to F-off last week (true story, not proud)! *How is that perfect?*" I said.

She looked me straight in the eye and said, "Yeah, but you always make it right," and she burst into fresh tears.

I share this story to illustrate how we don't have to do the right thing *all* the time. Clearly, telling your 14-year-old daughter to F-off in the heat of an argument is not something I would ever advocate.

But there is always, *always,* room for personal responsibility.

To me, this is the practice. This is what we commit to when we decide to parent with Joyful Courage. We own our shit. We make it right. While our children may find this incredibly annoying, we still do it. And in doing so, we model a powerful life skill.

That afternoon, I said to my daughter, "Making it right is not something I am willing to stop doing. I am not perfect, far from it, but I will always take responsibility when I am hurtful to someone else."

She went on to let me know that sometimes *I* am ready to make amends before *she* is ready to go there. This was powerful information for me. *I* may be ready to own my actions, but *she* may still be hurting and not yet ready.

Joyful Courage gives me the humility I need to take this feedback and let it inform and inspire my future interactions with her.

And all of this requires me to be in the moment and to be connected to myself (breath, body, balcony) so I can hear what my child is sharing with me from a place of openness and nonjudgment.

As we move into the final section of this book, I invite you to check in with yourself and explore what you are taking away so far. What is landing for you? What questions keep popping up? What is your inner voice telling you?

Checking in like this is something we should *always* be doing. It allows us to be observing ourselves and our learning. It allows us to leave our autopilot at the door and to reflect on what is true for us in that moment.

Sometimes when we are learning something new and trying it on for size, we expect it to be easy. And then when it isn't, we get all up in our head about what a failure we are.

I want to be super clear here—the goal with all of this work is to try to be *better*, to show up better for our children and the people we love. *Never, ever, is the message that if you aren't perfect, you are failing.*

Never.

Mistakes are a gift. Mistakes teach us so much about ourselves, and they highlight where we can continue to grow and develop.

You won't always remember to find your breath. Some days you will choose to stay in your head, and the conversation you have will be about your ungrateful, little-shit kids. The balcony seat will sometimes only be an afterthought, when it's too late.

It's okay.

What I do invite you to do, each and every day, is to be *reflective*, to be *responsible*, to *own your stuff*. Because this matters just as much as doing the work to stay present, loving, and available in the moment.

Control Is an Illusion.

If you are a self-identified control freak, I get you! Parenting, for me, has been the ultimate lesson in how to let go, to realize that control is an illusion.

What does it mean to let go?

I have a picture on the wall in my office that says, "Whatever you can't control is teaching you how to let go." I look at this often and consider all the layers of "letting go."

This has been the biggest thing I've learned as a parent. In the end, if I control everything, how will they grow and develop into adults who can navigate their own lives?

And yet, OMG, letting go is so *hard*.

If I am being totally honest, I thought I had the whole control thing under control. I really believed that I had dealt with it, recognized my own limitations and moved on.

Then my oldest sank into the teen years.

Holy cow!

Here is what I think is important to keep in mind as we learn to let go—*know how to fill the gap*. When we hold on to control, we are holding on to *something*, even if it is an illusion.

When you let go of control, you might feel like you're free falling, as though there isn't anything to keep you anchored.

It's so uncomfortable! Sometimes even straight-up painful.

Because that's how it feels, we often snap back to our controlling ways. It is just too scary, too unsettling, too unfamiliar to not feel as though we "have it handled."

This is where we can choose *trust*.

Redefining trust.

We have to trust that our kids can handle hurt, disappointment, and pain. We have to trust that giving them space to do all of this will teach them that they are capable and resilient.

We have to trust that our kids will learn from their mistakes. We have to trust that the relationship we grow and nurture with them is enough.

We have to trust that staying calm, taking care of ourselves, and avoiding the emotional freight train matters.

I'm not suggesting we throw up our hands and watch our kids head down self-destructive paths. Instead, I am offering you the opportunity to relax a bit, and to remember that life's lessons can be powerful when we're able to get out of the way.

Here are some stories about this from the Joyful Courage community:

"I was pouring the wholesale-sized syrup into a smaller container when I realized I needed to clean the container lid. I asked my seven-year-old to watch the container as I walked 10 seconds away. He knocked into the table and the syrup spilled all over. He jumped up screaming that he was so dumb. I held him and said, 'It's a mistake. I am here.'

He raged about what an idiot he was and even said he wanted to kill himself. I empathized, 'Those are some big feelings, huh? This mistake feels so big right now. You can ride this wave, you can handle it.' He cried and ranted some more. Then he went to be alone.

I cleaned up the syrup and when he came back down, I asked him if he noticed anything about the table. I said, 'There is no evidence of syrup anywhere. I want to tell you: no mistake is bigger than my love for you.'

He fell into my arms and I held him. 'Would it make sense that since half the bottle of syrup spilled, I should then empty out the rest of the syrup onto the carpet, destroying the table **and** *the carpet?' He looked at me like I was crazy and said no.*

'No mistake is worth your life,' I said. 'Don't make permanent decisions about temporary problems. The big wave will pass and you will be okay.' He smiled and ran off to play. It's possible he did not understand that concept (being seven years old), yet it's a seed. It will grow in time. He likely responded to my relaxed way of discussing it and knew it was all going to be okay."

– Mama Liz N.

"My seven-year-old son (Grade 2) had two weeks off school for spring break. At the beginning of the break, I asked him what his plan was for doing his reading homework over the break. He was noncommittal, but he said, 'I'll do it—just not right now.' I said that was fine as long as he understood it was up to him to make a plan to do the reading. He was happy with that and I didn't push it. I made a decision not to remind him about it at all.

Two weeks went by, and before we knew it, spring break was just about over. The day before we went back, I said, 'Have you made sure your backpack is all ready for tomorrow?' And that's when he remembered. He ended up using all of his evening free time reading his French books to me. A few times he said he didn't know if he would be able to do it, and I agreed that it was a lot of reading.

He actually was able to complete it in time, but it was a lot of work, and while he was in the middle of it he had to face the possibility that he might have to explain to his teacher that he didn't do his work. I was really impressed by his motivation and determination to do it. He really took responsibility for it and didn't once ask me why I didn't remind him."

– Mama Christie P.

Let's put letting go and trusting into perspective. Below, I am going to share wisdom that was shared with me by my dear friend and parent educator, Sahara Pirie. Sahara is a Positive Discipline Lead Trainer and has been working with parents and parent educators in the Seattle area for close to 20 years. She created a visual that puts the whole conversation about "boundaries" into perspective.

Kids typically come to us as babies, and we hold our babies close. We nurture them, feed them, take care of them.

As they grow into toddlers, we keep their environment safe, putting away anything that could hurt them. We allow them to explore, while keeping a watchful eye. We watch them navigating the world, trusting that, with practice, they will find strength in those wobbly legs and eventually learn to go up and down the stairs.

We give our preschoolers even more space, while still under our supervision. They may learn to use more tools, explore a little further out into the yard. We offer them trust and encouragement as they wave to us from the top of the big slide on the playground. We may catch our breath, but we know it is important for them to know what they can do, to begin to trust their own judgement.

As our children move into the school age years, we look for opportunities to teach, model, and practice life skills with them. We support them in problem solving with friends and siblings. We love them through their losses, celebrate with them through their wins—trusting that they will hear the message around the importance of "It doesn't matter if you win or lose; it's how you play the game."

The middle school years take our children out of our protective cocoon. They move into a new era and they may not always share with us what is going on. Gah! It is hard but appropriate. Self-awareness becomes ever more present, and the perception of their peers takes on greater importance. If our children haven't invited us to let go yet, it often shows up here.

And then our children morph into something new. The high school years arrive. The boundaries we have set are still there, but they have expanded. Our teenagers show up to those boundaries with ladders, pickaxes, and wire cutters—eager to push and pull, and to learn from the experience of experimenting with where the boundaries hold firm and where they give.

Holy guacamole.

I know there are all sorts of variables in the timelines I just shared—where we live, family systems, choices in the kind of schooling our kids receive, etc., but through it all, we must learn to let go and trust our children.

I have learned that "I trust you to never do anything stupid or risky" doesn't make sense, and sets me and my child up for failure.

Teenagers are wired to do stupid and risky things.

No matter how much we track them or monitor them (thank you, smart phones), like every generation of teens before them (including us, of course), they will find ways to engage in the stupid and the risky.

So, what I now am working on is *trusting that my children will learn from their mistakes.* I trust they don't need me to point out all the places they get it wrong. This is hard. Especially when I am emotionally triggered, feel a loss of control, and *want to point all those places out to them....*

So, I choose to practice the Three Bs. Finding my breath, dropping into my body, and taking the balcony seat to get more perspective. I practice letting go. I practice trust.

Our children are on their own paths. They need us to create boundaries and guidelines, yes, but they also need us to give them room to explore the world, and they need us to stay calm—and *not* freak out—when they inevitably screw up.

Our children need us to *choose in* to our practice.

CHAPTER EIGHT

You Have the Tools,
Now Stay Out of the Station

So, in the writing of this book, I was invited to look at the phrase "choosing in." The people who were supporting me really didn't want me to use those two words together. They felt like you, the reader, wouldn't know exactly what it was I was talking about.

But I decided to keep those two words in this book. Because I feel like we are always being invited to *choose in* to the practice of being the parent we want to be.

If it is new to you to hear those two words together, I simply invite you to play with it. I invite you to consider that you do have a choice here. That it is a choosing *in*. Just like we dive *into* a pool, we choose *into* the parenting practice that we believe in. We choose *into* the experiences that we want to have.

Choosing in to our practice is saying yes. Yes to discomfort. Yes to trust. Yes to the unknown.

Choosing in to our practice is being willing to breathe through our triggers. Being willing to take the time we need to feel our body, slow down our heartbeat, find our peace, our calm, our connection. Choosing in is trusting that how we show up matters.

Choosing in to our practice is actually taking the time to use the Three Bs: Breath. Body. Balcony—even when everything inside of us is telling us something different.

Remember earlier in this book when I shared about the list of challenges I presented to the parents in my parenting workshops, and how as a result we are reminded that we don't live in our own private freakshow?

There is a second list that the parents help to create during my classes as well. I invite parents to imagine that their child is now in their late twenties and comes home for a visit. When they open the door, what qualities do they hope their child (now an adult) has developed?

Here is what shows up, every time:

- Respectful
- Responsible
- Honest
- Patient
- Compassionate
- Empathetic
- Kind
- Self-advocating
- Accountable
- Hardworking
- Healthy
- Adventurous
- Flexible
- Leader
- Self-regulated
- Creative
- Self-aware

It is so powerful to get a clear vision of what we want most for our children. And again, these are universal: all parents want their children to grow into these skills.

How do kids learn? *They learn through our example.*

So, consider how *you* want to experience life.

What happens when we decide to be the creators of our own experience? What happens when we decide we are going to take charge of our life and become independent from the external experiences that occur around us?

We're empowered.

It changes everything to move through the world knowing you influence your experience. When you decide you have the ultimate say in how you feel, you release the other person to their own experience. You're no longer in a dance of power that leaves you and the other person feeling spent and disconnected.

And isn't this what we hope for our children? That they begin to realize how they affect the way that life plays out for them? That they are the heroes they have been waiting for?

Here is what I heard from the Joyful Courage community about choosing into the practice of Joyful Courage and being empowered:

> *Every morning I have a choice to give my power away by blaming outside people, events, or circumstances, and letting them dictate my mood and reactions, to stand in my power and choose how I want to show up. Choosing in to my practice includes using as many tools as I need to create connection, not only with my kids, but also with myself."*

> – *Mama Anna P.*

*"Choosing in is deciding each moment to **be** intentional. To trust myself and my kids. When I make a mistake, I choose in to finding grace and trying again, and again. Choosing in is understanding that this is a practice, not something to perfect. Choosing in is to be intentional about supporting myself so that I can support others."*

– Mama Monica Z.

"Choosing in means having a deep appreciation for my kids, for who they are even when it isn't convenient for me. It means them knowing how much I love them, unconditionally, through my actions, words, body language, and connection...and then reconnecting and owning up to my mistakes when I make them."

– Mama Justine S.

*"Choosing in to Joyful Courage means that I continue to learn and practice new and old tools; it is a **yes** to the fact that this is a long-term journey and that I am choosing this path even though it can feel unfamiliar or new to me."*

– Mama Heidi B.

Choosing in to your practice is surrendering to trust. Letting go releases the grip that fear has on us.

Every single life experience adds to the tapestry that is us. Every experience has the potential to grow us. Even the really horrible things that happen.

This is hard for me to write as I consider that painful, abusive experiences have occurred in the lives of so many people, and maybe even you. What opens up when we can say, "Yes, that happened to me, and I can move forward as an ever more complete person, because I am a survivor of that pain"?

I have shared a little about my experience with my mom growing up. When I decided to leave her and move in with my father at 15 years old, I was hurting. And while I was so grateful and so privileged to have had the love and support I received at my father's house, the pain of what felt like losing my mom was there.

And the guilt. I had left my mom. I knew that she was hurting and that I was the cause. I had left my younger siblings there as well. And yet, I was so glad to be exactly where I was, that I had been brave enough to do what I needed to do. It was really difficult to hold all of that at fifteen years old.

Plus, I was a teenager, and I got really good at pushing the hard emotions down and not dealing with them. I was receiving messages that I wasn't supposed to let what was happening between my mom and I become an excuse. So, I carried on. And as time went by, my mom and I became more and more distant.

My "formative years" passed by. I went to college and lived my life, did my own individuating and experimenting with figuring out who I was in the world.

Long story short, I grew up.

My younger sister ended up going to college close to where I was living. She was an all-American softball star, and my mom would come up and watch her play ball. We slowly reconnected, but the void that had been created in our relationship was evident to us both. I knew I wanted a relationship with my mom, and I was willing to let go of all the hurt and pain from my teen years.

I became pregnant with my daughter. This was the first of many times that my daughter would be the facilitator of healing for my mother and me. I knew I wanted my mom to be at the birth, and I also knew that she would need to be educated in the choices I was making (natural birth, midwife, birth center).

It was so comforting to have her be a part of my experience of becoming a mom. It was as if she got to know who I was through understanding the choices I was making.

We were rebuilding our relationship. And while there was never an acknowledgement of our past hurts, we were moving forward. As much as I wanted to hear an apology, or something, from my mom, I was also willing to let it go if it meant we could move forward.

And every once in a while, she would make a comment to let me know that she was aware of the mistakes of the past, but I came to realize that it was incredibly difficult for her to confront that time. Being a mother now, I imagine that the guilt and shame of how things played out weighs heavily on her. I have found compassion for her experience, and I no longer let the past get in my way.

As I have demonstrated throughout this book, the process of showing up to life and parenting in a way that is vulnerable and authentic—choosing in to Joyful Courage—takes work. And in my own story, that work started with forgiving my mom. Not only forgiving my mom, but also acknowledging that it is because of and inside my past experiences with her, that I find my passion for working with parents today.

I am grateful for it all. I am grateful that I am the one, the mother who said "yes!" to being more aware of how I am showing up to my experience.

And as I stated earlier, it is my relationship with my daughter that is continuing to facilitate healing between me and my mom. It brings tears to my eyes when I consider how the ways that I am vulnerable about *my* parenting opens the space for my mom to step into *her* vulnerability. We are making things right with each other. No regrets. Always looking forward.

And that is what can happen when we *choose* not to let old pain and hurt be in the driver's seat.

That is what can happen when we *choose* to nurture that hurt child inside of us, and move to a place of love and compassion, releasing resentment and anger for the events that we had no control over.

We become free.

While your story is different than my story, and it may be harder or easier for you to navigate the hurt you are carrying, what I am hoping you are opening up to is that it *is* possible to heal.

Of course, I recognize that choosing to let go of deep hurt requires more than reading this book. Personally, I have participated in many types of personal growth and learning and they each help in their own way. And we learn from each other, and each other's experiences.

Be a yes to learning and watch your life change.

Finding lightness.

It's important to keep coming back to how the experience of the emotional freight train *feels* because this is how we learn to know that we are *on* it.

Typically, when we are on the train, it is because whatever we are reacting to feels so big and heavy. We find ourselves in a space of urgency and we feel the need to *do* something.

What if we were able to find some *lightness* in those hot and heavy moments? What if we could literally *lighten up*, change our energy, and shake off all that weight that can feel so suffocating?

Lightness is a tool.

Lightness is release.

Lightness is trust.

Lightness is allowing an experience to happen.

What do I mean by that?

Resistance is at the root of most suffering. Whenever we resist something, we find ourselves caught up in our emotions. Sometimes on the parenting journey, we resist the stage of development our child is going through, or we resist letting go of our vision for how something *should* go. Sometimes we resist our child's need for autonomy, or their bad mood.

Any time we *resist* what is happening, we suffer. In that suffering we can find ourselves on the train simply to pass around the pain we are feeling in the moment.

Now you may be thinking: Well, what if my child is doing drugs, or lying, or stealing??? Don't we want to resist that?

No, you don't. Please don't.

The opposite of resisting is accepting. Accepting is the first step in recovery. Acceptance opens the door to compassion. Acceptance allows space for possibilities.

But what we resist, persists.

Let's look at it another way...

Have you ever had the experience of having a perfectly fine day, only to be greeted by a really grumpy partner? Maybe they come home and toss their stuff around the kitchen, ranting about their crummy boss or the jerk who cut them off? What do you notice happening inside of *you*?

Then maybe your kids walk in and are a bit whinier than normal, demanding this or that from you. Are you able to stay calm and connected to yourself, and respond to your child in a way that is helpful and kind?

Maybe?

Maybe not?

Who do we blame for snapping at our children? That grumpy-ass partner, dammit.

I easily fall into this cycle when I am not paying attention to my internal experience. I allow my partner's energy to cause me pain or suffering or heaviness. I am resistant to compassion or meeting my kids where they are at. With that in my body, am I moving towards lightness? Heck no—I respond to my child by passing on the pain and suffering that is going on for me!!

I know it can feel like I'm talking in circles but bear with me. The scenario above is one that plays out over and over when we aren't in the present moment. It highlights the ways that we hop on our train, or other people's trains, without realizing what we're doing.

What if this wasn't a metaphor? Could you imagine all the times we would look around and realize that we were in a whole new town with all the train hopping we do?

Lightness can be used when we are getting pulled into the energy of the people around us and we choose to rise above it; we choose to bounce up and out. It can be an internal conversation that sounds like, "Wait a minute, this is yours, not mine."

I recently had the opportunity to practice this when I was in the backyard one morning, finishing up some self care, and my son poked his head out the door and stated, "There are no bagels!"

He was visibly irritated and I could feel the blame he was throwing my way. I paused, deciding not to say anything at all. He rolled his eyes in exasperation and closed the door.

I took a few breaths as I gathered my things, put a smile on my face, and found some curiosity. I went into the house and saw him sitting on the couch. "Sorry there were no bagels," I said. "Can you figure out something to eat? Do you need me to list off what is available? What do you need from me right now?"

This was so helpful; it allowed the tension to leave the space between us, and he responded by saying he would find something to eat.

This could have turned into something very different had I responded to the heaviness that came with his first comment. I could have gone on and on, defensively, about how there was plenty to eat, and what was his problem, and didn't he know how privileged he was??? Pain and suffering. I am glad I used lightness that morning.

"When I am able to reach for lightness, I feel like I am setting the right example for my children. Not everything is a serious travesty! If I can be light, many potential conflicts or problems just melt away, and my family feels more connected."

— Mama Lauren R.

"Lightness has helped me remember that laughter, fun, humor, play, and presence are all so important to my kids, and can often create stronger paths for communication than anything else."

— Mama Justine S.

"When I think of 'lightness' as a tool, I see it as a way to keep me grounded in myself. I am a bit different. I have been told by many people throughout my life that I just see things differently. And I think that has to do with my internal 'lightness,' what I call 'whimsy.' I enjoy making tasks fun and playful. I think that my parenting journey is helping me return to my whimsical center, to let go a little, and to stop taking things so seriously. As I turn to this lightness, I feel more sure of myself, which helps me hold space for the stress my children are experiencing. It helps them find themselves, and bring themselves back to their center in their own ways."

— Mama Nelly B.

Lightness can be evoked. Once we realize we are carrying the baggage of pain and suffering, we can put it down to lighten the load. To do this, we turn to the body.

Using our body to shift.

I have had mothers show up to my workshops feeling that they have been duped. They feel like the motherhood experience that society sold them was not the experience they've found themselves having. They feel exhausted, angry, sad, and they have a tremendous amount of guilt for feeling this way.

They are carrying the heavy baggage of pain and suffering.

As you know, I was in my own pain and suffering experience as my oldest child moved into her first few months of high school. She was expanding who she was, trying things on, pushing back, making mistakes. The baggage that I was carrying was heavy.

The hardest part about this was the way that my daughter pushed me away. It felt as though every time I saw her in her pain and tried to connect with her, she would shut me out.

This hurt. This was also, on some levels, developmentally appropriate.

I was resistant to the fact that I was being invited to let go, share the power, and allow her space to explore her world. This was what she needed, yet I would often find myself in resistance.

Why do we go there? Why do we try and take control?

Why?????

Because we are human. When we feel threatened, unsafe, or because at some level our sense of connection and adequacy is feeling vulnerable, we go into fight-or-flight mode. We care deeply about those we love the most, so it makes sense that they are the ones who can invite us into feeling this way.

Okay, great. So, what do we do about it?

There are some things that I have done...

I have been to therapy. I have had life coaching and parent coaching. I am surrounded by people who are resources that support me in making sense of what I am experiencing.

I have an energy worker that I *love*. She shows me the places where my soul is holding onto generational trauma.

I love transformational workshops—I love to insert myself into experiences that allow me to see myself from the inside out. I seek out these experiences.

I meditate regularly and I am an avid journaler. I take care of myself.

And still there are times when the emotional freight train pulls into the station...

And my favorite practice for supporting myself was introduced in the last chapter. The Three Bs: Breath. Body. Balcony.

Let's take a moment to practice putting the three Bs together. Are you ready?

Bring your attention to your breath. Allow yourself to inhale and exhale.

Notice the muscles in your face right now. Bring your attention there, and really explore what is happening around your eyes, in your forehead, in your jaw. Imagine with every breath you take that you can soften the muscles in your face.

Now drop into your neck and shoulders, and notice the tension there. Is there room for your shoulders to drop down and back? Try it and see how it feels. Release any tightness with your breath.

Do you see how your heart opens, simply by pulling back your shoulders a little? Now take a breath and imagine that fresh new air going straight into your heart center. What is your experience? If you are thinking that it is random of me to ask that, close your eyes for a bit and take 10 slow breaths straight into your heart center, and then reflect on what you notice.

Now drop your attention into your belly and your booty, and see what is calling to be let go of. We hold so much of our fear in our hips and butts—what happens when we let it go?

With the next few breaths, feel your connection to the ground beneath you. Feel the support of your legs and feet as they hold you up and root you to the earth.

Now smile…

Imagine that you have put down the heavy baggage of pain and suffering. You have released them. They are now moving away from you, on the emotional freight train that they came on.

Notice what is available when we start with the body, when we open up our hearts, when we release the tension. Feel what is happening for you. Imagine what becomes available inside of relationship when we practice noticing what is happening in our body and *allow* for our intended way of being—not *thinking* about that way of being but really *embodying* the space for that way of being to exist.

Imagine what you would see from the balcony seat. Find an audio of this exercise on my website, www.joyfulcourage.com/eftbook

"When I use the Three Bs, I am able to stop the chatter in my mind and listen to what my child is trying to tell me about his experience. I am able to put aside all the feelings I have and take some time to listen to his perspective."

– Mama Christie P.

"My oldest expressed that he felt his sisters were getting longer bedtimes than he was, and that it wasn't fair. My first thought was how he was contributing to that issue, and if only he would.... But then I was able to take a balcony seat and see that I could be celebrating the fact that he was able to articulate his feelings to me. I got curious and tried to see it from his point of view. He wasn't trying to be difficult at bedtime; he just wasn't getting his needs met."

– Mama Lauren R.

To avoid the emotional freight train, we have to choose in to *using* the tools. We have to say, "Now I will choose to show up differently for my children" and try something new. We have to explore the Three Bs and trust that keeping ourselves grounded, present, and openminded will support us in the long term.

This is bigger than reading this book. This is actually putting the concepts I am sharing into practice on a regular basis to *stay off the emotional freight train* on your parenting journey.

Using your body as a tool makes a huge difference. When you practice *embodying* the ways of beings that you want most, you will find them much easier to access.

So how do we make this sustainable? Let's move into the last chapter to discuss this.

CHAPTER NINE

The Continuing Journey of Joyful Courage

All right, so maybe it is a stretch for you to consider that shifting your body is enough to get you off the crazy train.

Let's just remember what fight or flight, which is basically our response when we are on the train, is good for:

- When someone's immediate safety is threatened.

Yup, that is pretty much all I've got. Safety. If your child is running out on the busy road, yes, please kick it into gear and save him.

If there is a wild animal coming after your family, please let that crazy train energy take over and do what you need to do to fight off the beast!

But here is the deal: Most of the time the challenges that show up in parenting are NOT emergencies. We just respond to them as if they were.

You may be thinking, "But wait a minute, Casey, aren't' some fights with our children worth having?"

I am here to say that *nothing* can be accomplished when we are in fight-or-flight mode. Does that mean that we *don't have* heated discussions and disagreements? No. We won't get through our parenting journey without lively and sometimes tense conversations. But holding boundaries or standing up for your values are not the same as fighting.

When asked about the challenges that trigger her emotional freight train, mama Tricia shared that it is *"often tied up with events where my children are not 'listening' to me or not completing the tasks that need to be completed at a given time or for a given activity....When my children are excessively whiny or sometimes even excessively exuberant....When the kids make or have made a mess."*

Again, when we feel threatened or out of control, our ancient survival skills show up as the emotional freight train, and we respond to our children and their behavior *as if they were the bear trying to kill us.*

Most of what our children's behavior is can be boiled down to two things:

1. Lacking skills to handle their situation

2. Misinterpretation of connection, significance, or influence

So, think about it this way: When your child was first learning to walk, did you find yourself getting all frustrated that they weren't masters of balance? When they took a few steps and then fell down, did you roll your eyes and consider that they might be "playing you?" When they got better at walking but still would sometimes choose to crawl, did you think they were just being defiant or looking for attention?

No. You didn't. That would be ridiculous.

Our children are developing skills over time and through the experiences they are having. They are making lots of mistakes (and so are we).

Sometimes, when their "mistakes" leave us feeling embarrassed, fearful, or angry, we respond to them as a threat.

But this book isn't about them; it's about *you*.

And, I might add, you are also continuing to develop new skills here, and you will make lots of mistakes. So, let's talk about how to set you up for success.

Support yourself.

If we want to make lasting change in our lives, we do the following:

1. Declare it

2. Practice it

3. Revisit it

Declare it.

You are ready to go. You are ready to embrace Joyful Courage and show up as best you can for yourself and others.

Put it down on paper, say it out loud, find a partner or friend who will listen, and spell it out for them.

Take it from your head and put it out into the universe! It is amazing what can happen when we declare what we want.

I am partial to Post-it Notes. I have them all around my world. They say things like "listen deeply," and "connect through the eyes," and "time is abundant." They are little reminders of the ways I want to live and the beliefs I want to embody. The other three humans in my home see those notes too. While they may not be conscious of it, they are receiving the messages.

Practice it.

The other tool that I love, besides Post-it Notes, is the reminder app on my phone. When I am working on a deep practice of love, or trust, or surrender, or lightness, I set reminders throughout the day so that I am prompted to take a moment, or many, to drop into my body and invite in what I want most.

You have heard me talk about "what's familiar" throughout this book. We will continue to go to what is familiar till the day we die. If what is familiar is *annoyed*, that is where we will go; if it's *resentful*, that is where we will go. If we want something different, then we have to *practice* something different. We have to teach ourselves a new familiar.

Practice bringing curiosity alive in your body on a regular basis, and it will teach your body to become more familiar with it. The same is true for gratitude, love, kindness—remind yourself to *feel* these throughout the day.

Revisit it.

Every new practice gets old, right? It doesn't matter if we are talking about diet, exercise, doing more reading for fun, or shifting how we show up in parenting. The farther away we get from the big "declaration," the more the motivation wears off.

A simple remedy for this is to simply make time to revisit what we want most—and why we want it—regularly. This could be a weekly self check-in, or perhaps daily for a while. Consider: Why are you making time for this practice? What do you need in order to choose in to Joyful Courage? Why is it important to you? And what is the progress you are making?

Reset it.

We all jump on the emotional freight train. We are human beings having a human experience, and it is full of *other* humans doing the same. Life can be a shit show sometimes, and that is okay.

When you find yourself out of your practice, when you come up for air and notice that you have been riding the train way more than you want to, it is time to *reset.*

Go back to the start. Declare what you want. Rewrite your reminders.

Celebrate it.

Enough with the perfectionism. Even when the shit hits the fan and it feels as though the world is on a mission to take you down, find some celebration. Your growing awareness about your own response to your children's behavior is a step in the right direction. Yay! Own that.

What am I talking about, you ask?

Every single moment is an opportunity to learn and grow, and to lean in, and to try to be our best. We don't always see every moment as an opportunity, but what if we did?

What if when our toddler is throwing (another) fit, kicking, and screaming, we say to ourselves, "Awesome, I get to practice patience right now. Thank you, my little toddler." Or what if when our tween freezes us out, we say, "Okay, this is my chance to practice letting go and trusting." How would that serve us?

I know this is a tall order, but even if we could greet *some* of the challenges in our lives with a celebration, wouldn't that make a difference?

Try it.

Creating Systems.

Systems and routines work for the grownups too. And our willingness to set them up for ourselves will directly impact how deep we go in this work.

I mentioned already that I use Post-it Notes and setting reminders. They work. The point of it is to practice what we want when the risk is low. Don't wait for the epic kid meltdown to practice the Three Bs, or you will have a hard time accessing them.

Make it a habit to practice just before you get in the car, or in the grocery store checkout line, or every day at 2 p.m.

Practice going through the process of bringing your attention to your breath, noticing your body, and taking the balcony seat.

If you are working on a certain way of being, like playful, or kind, or brave, then when you are in the body part of the practice, imagine that the way of being is a light that is at first only a speck, and with every breath it grows into a bigger and bigger ball of light, expanding in your body. Notice what happens when you are full of playful. Notice what your body posture moves toward when you are growing in kindness.

When you move to the balcony seat, you are seeing not only from a broader, bigger perspective, you are also looking through the lens of kindness, you are seeing how playfulness can be helpful. Go to www.joyfulcourage.com/eftbook for some guided audio to support you in your learning.

So yes, creating systems and routines for practicing the work when the train *is not* in the station is powerful.

Meditation.

I encourage clients to practice meditation regularly. Meditation strengthens the mindfulness muscles. Meditation supports us in coming back to the present moment time and time again.

One time, when talking about meditation with a dear friend, I told her I had a hard time having an empty mind when I meditate.

Her response changed everything for me.

She said, *"Casey, meditation isn't about having an empty mind; meditation is the practice of recognizing when your mind is full, and coming back to breath, back to the present moment."*

Gold.

Isn't that exactly what we need most when we are on the emotional freight train? We need to know we are on it. Then we can choose to get off it. It's about practice and wearing down a new path.

Journaling.

I am also a big fan of journaling. Journaling is an effective way to check in with your practice, to celebrate your progress, and to ask questions when you feel stuck.

But I don't like to write! Fine, don't use complete sentences—use bullet points, or draw a picture. This is yours. This is a place that needs to be useful for *you.* Spelling doesn't count here, nor does content, really. Sometimes all I do in my journal is a great big brain dump. Or I may use it to vent. Or I may simply spend five minutes writing questions.

The main thing to remember is that there are no rules here. What I *will* say is that using your journal to beat yourself up or blame the world for your problems is *not* helpful. When you find yourself getting blamey, go through and find all the places where you can take personal responsibility for your current situation. Use it to move toward growth and solutions.

Some of the parents I work with meditate/journal in the morning before the family is up (and this is my favorite time). Some do it before bed; others find time in the middle of the day. The important thing here is that you fold it into *your* day so it happens.

Sleep.

For me, getting up in the morning for my quiet time requires that I pay attention to when I am going to bed. Sleep matters, people! If you get less that seven hours (I really wanted to write eight there) you need to do something about it. Do it. It will become a mental health issue, no matter how much coffee you drink.

Movement.

Movement matters too. You don't need to do crossfit or yoga every day, but you do need to *move*. This can be a walk around the block, a dance around the kitchen, stretching on the living room floor. The important thing is that you move your body. When you move your body, you are also moving energy, and you are releasing places that are stuck.

A healthy body supports a healthy mind and healthy emotions.

There is time, I promise you. Just take stock of what you are already doing and get creative.

To live an intentional life, you have to create an intentional practice. What I love about this is that it is available to everyone.

Make it a regular practice to choose the Three Bs: Breath. Body. Balcony.

Declare what you will do, then practice it, revisit it, reset it, and celebrate it!

I encourage you to begin to take care of yourself in a way that is meaningful. Take care of your soul. Meditation, journaling, sleep, movement. This will support you in creating a sustainable shift in your parenting.

This is the end of the book, and the beginning of a new practice. I also invite you to reread this book. Now that you are at the end of the book, you have a different lens than you had at the beginning.

You're amazing, and you are exactly the right parent for your child.

Acknowledgements

Thank you first to my family. Rowan and Ian, you give me ample content for sharing about the parenting journey. Everything we grow through together shapes me into an ever-better supporter of the parents I work with. You two are everything and I thank the universe every day that you chose me to be your mom. Ben, you are my rock. Thank you for encouraging me, and celebrating me, and supporting me through my self-doubt and discouragement. You are my favorite person and I love you so much.

Thank you to my parents. I am eternally grateful for you, and all the ways you loved me and grew me into the person that I am today. Dad and Julie, thank you for being there for me when I needed you most. Thank you for fostering a work ethic and belief in myself that I could do anything I set my mind to (including writing a book). Mom, thank you so much for being willing to grow with me on my journey. I love you so much and am so grateful for all of the twist and turns, ups and downs. Thank you for being open, and for seeing me and loving me, and encouraging me in all the ways that you do.

Thank you to the Joyful Courage community—OMG, you people are so amazing. Special thanks to the bonfire circle—Christie, Nelly, Liz, Lauren, Heidi, Tricia, Monica, Justine, Ana, Elizabeth. You gals have grown me as a guide, and educator, and human being. I am so honored to know each one of you and in awe of your commitment to showing up as your best for your family. You are AMAZING.

To all of my supporters at Book Launchers—Tim, Jaqueline, and Julie—THANK YOU. Thank you for your kindness, the funny memes, the perfectly timed encouraging emails. Thank you for seeing this book as something that the world needed to read.

Thank you to all that have come before me and inspired me to write this book, Jane Nelsen, your work with Positive Discipline changed the life of my family and gave me purpose. Jody McVittie, your mentorship has grown me as a mother, facilitator and human, thank you for opening me up to the world of transformation and embodiment. To all of my beautiful friend and colleagues who read and reviews this book, especially Dr. Tina Bryson, who responded enthusiastically with a blurb for the cover, thank you, thank you thank you. You encourage me daily and I am so honored to walk with you on this journey.

And YOU. You bought the book, have read all the way to the end. Thank YOU for trusting that I have something useful to share. I am honored to do the work I do and to serve you. Thank you for continuing to listen to the podcast, show up in the FB group, and support me in all the ways that you do. We are all in this together!